SATHYA NAMBIRAJAN

Finding Home

An Indian family's journey to Germany

First edition

Cover art by Vidhya Hariharan
Editing by Claude.ai
Editing by Chat GPT
Editing by Williams Rajkumar

This book was professionally typeset on Reedsy.
Find out more at reedsy.com

To our adorable daughter Ranjana

Contents

Foreword

Foreword 01 - Sumithra

When I began reading Sathya Nambirajan's book, I must admit that I had certain preconceptions about what their writing would be like. Initially, I expected a self-centered, boastful, and materialistic autobiography of two individuals who had left their homeland in pursuit of new experiences and cultures. That was my biased opinion about people who migrate, and I was prepared to read a story that would reinforce those stereotypes.

However, within a few pages, I was pleasantly surprised to discover that the authors are seasoned souls who share their life journey with wit, whimsy, and wisdom. They masterfully convey their experiences, imparting valuable insights and lessons learned along the way. As I continued reading, I found myself enthralled by their stories, which were far from the self-centered and materialistic narrative I had initially expected.

As someone who once viewed the term 'Indian diaspora' as a euphemism for 'brain drain,' I finally found solace in their works. I realized that the concept of brain drain is often tied to the divisions among us, and that their writing conveyed a powerful alternative. Through their stories, I came to understand the true essence of *'Vasudhaiva Kutumbakam,'* a phrase from the Maha Upanishad that means 'The world is one family.' The whole verse goes like this:

'*ayam bandhurayam neti ganana laghuchetasam udaracharitanam tu vasudhaiva kutumbakam*'

'*One is a relative; the other is a stranger. For those who live magnanimously the entire world constitutes but a family.*'

This ancient wisdom resonated deeply, and I began to see the diaspora experience in a new light.

The authors' native literature is replete with beautiful phrases that resonate deeply with the aforementioned wisdom. One such phrase, *'Yaadhum oorae yaavarum kelir,'* translates to 'Every city is my own city, and every person is my relative.' A beautiful expression of universal kinship, emphasizing that we are all connected and part of a larger human family. This inclusive sentiment is further underscored by another phrase, *'Thiraikkadal odiyum thiraviyam thedu,'* which, on the surface, means 'To gain wealth, one can travel across the ocean.' However, its deeper significance is that to seek the true meaning of life or gain wisdom, one can courageously venture beyond the familiar, even if it means crossing oceans. It is a poignant reminder that true growth and understanding often require us to venture beyond our comfort zones and embrace the unknown.

By now it will be easy to assume that this book is solely focused on spiritual awareness, given the themes and phrases I've mentioned. However, the truth is that it's also remarkably trendy in many ways. The authors' exploration of childhood trauma and traveling, for instance, resonates with the current social media buzz around these topics. The book's unique blend of spirituality, personal growth, and modern relevance makes it a fascinating read.

Both authors have experienced their fair share of trauma in childhood and young adulthood, with one author facing the devastating loss of a loved one and the other enduring a severe natural calamity.

The authors have shown remarkable courage in sharing their personal struggles, without sugarcoating their achievements or shying away from revealing their socioeconomic background. They have openly discussed their traumas, demonstrating a willingness to be vulnerable and authentic. This transparency is refreshing, as it acknowledges that success is not solely the result of individual merit, but also of circumstance and support. By sharing their stories, the authors have created a relatable and humanizing narrative that resonates with readers from diverse backgrounds. As Mitch Albom says, 'Never be ashamed of a scar. In the end, scars tell the story of our lives, everything that hurt us, and everything that healed us.'

Their stories reveal the long-lasting impact of these experiences, showcasing the transformative power of resilience in the face of adversity. Instead of letting challenges hinder their progress, they have skillfully turned every stumbling block into a stepping stone, leveraging their struggles to fuel personal growth and success. This remarkable ability to pivot and adapt is a testament to the human spirit's capacity for resilience and determination.

And the beautiful part of how the authors found each other is a testament to the power of love and connection. It reminded me of the quote again by my favorite writer, 'Sometimes, love brings you together, even as life keeps you apart!' This phrase perfectly captures the essence of the authors' journey, as they navigated life's challenges and distances, only to find each other in the most unexpected way. Their story is a heartwarming reminder that love can bridge even the widest of gaps and unite two souls in the most beautiful way.

Although the book is titled 'Finding Home', it also offers a wealth of information about the authors' traveling experiences, making it a valuable resource for both learners and explorers. The book's themes of self-discovery and personal growth are beautifully intertwined with stories of adventure and exploration, providing a unique and engaging reading experience.

What sets this book apart from a typical travel blog is its candid and balanced approach. The authors share not only the highlights and wonders of each travel destination but also the challenges and downsides, presenting a realistic and nuanced view of their experiences. This honest and informative narrative provides readers with a comprehensive understanding of what to expect, making it an invaluable resource for fellow travelers and adventurers.

Reading this book may be a therapeutic experience in itself, especially for those who resonate deeply with the authors' journeys. For others, it may serve as a catalyst for self-reflection and introspection, inviting readers to contemplate their own paths and celebrate their resilience in the face of adversity. As we ponder the challenges we've overcome, we're reminded that man-made struggles are, in fact, a part of the natural order, for humans are an integral part of nature - one that often forgets to nurture and care for itself.

The new generation can draw valuable lessons from this book, including the importance of simplicity, authenticity, and the healing power of arts. Through the authors' stories, they can discover how embracing simplicity can lead to a more fulfilling life, how being true to oneself can foster meaningful connections, and how creative expression can provide catharsis and solace. These real-life examples serve as a powerful reminder of the transformative impact of art on our well-being and the significance of staying true to ourselves.

In conclusion, home is more than just four walls and a roof - it's a sense of belonging, where we feel a deep connection with others as an extension of ourselves. As we read this book, we see reflections of ourselves in the authors' stories and realize that we are all interconnected, just like the famous Rumi quote says, 'You are not a drop in the ocean, you are the ocean in a drop.' This understanding reveals that our individual selves are part of a larger whole, and that the world is our shared home. May we embrace this unity and strive for peace and harmony, as the ancient Indian mantra says, '*Loka samastha sukhino bhavanthu*' which means 'may all beings live in peace and happiness!'

Foreword 02 - Berty Ashley

Picture this: two Tamil dreamers, with more grit than a dosa stone and more optimism than a mango tree in bloom, decide to pack their lives into suitcases and trade Tamilnadu's sunny chaos for Germany's brisk efficiency. What follows isn't just a story—it's a cinematic saga, equal parts rom-com, culture-clash drama, and motivational thriller.

'Finding Home' is not your average "life lessons with a side of dry toast" fare. It's a full-course Tamil-German fusion meal: spicy, hearty, and with just enough sauerkraut to keep you intrigued. The authors, who happen to also be each other's life partners, narrate their journey with such warmth and candor that you'll find yourself alternately laughing, crying, and Googling "how to do Gartenarbeitsschule in India".

Their story is one of resilience—of turning setbacks into setups for comebacks. From the relatable (dealing with a sense of purposelessness at work) to the unpredictable (wading through flooded streets at night to get to the police station), they've seen it all. And through it, they offer not just survival tips but thriving techniques for anyone contemplating a leap of faith.

This book is co-authored, and you can feel it in every page. One voice is peppered with Tamil idioms and humor, the other with reflective warmth and unshakeable practicality. Together, they form a duet—a conversational dance that's as entertaining as it is insightful. You're not reading their story; you're *watching* it unfold before you.

This isn't just a guide for Tamil couples or aspiring immigrants—it's for anyone who has ever faced the unknown with nothing but a dream and a backpack full of courage. It's for people who want to understand why certain challenges might make you stronger.

You'll pick up practical tips, sure, but you'll also find wisdom that transcends cultures: how to build a life together, even when the blueprint seems written in a language you don't speak.

The authors' journey is deeply inspiring, yes, but don't mistake this for a lecture. It's more like having a conversation with two exceptionally funny, slightly chaotic, and immensely lovable people who want nothing more than to share their joy of life with you. Their daughter, who I am sure will be a delightful blend of two rich cultures, is destined to become a tiny ambassador of their cross-continental love story—proving that home is where your family grows, regardless of the postal code.

You'll laugh. You'll learn. And if you're like me, you might even start planning your own move to Germany—though I'll admit, I'm mostly in it for the pretzels.

If you or someone you know is in a dilemma right now regarding moving away from home, remember the old Tamil idiom

> ‘முதல் படி சேகரிக்கும் தோழன் அவசியம்’
>
> (The first step requires a necessary friend)

Also give them this book. It will be that guiding friend.

Now, stop reading this foreword and dive into the book already. The good stuff awaits! Bon voyage.

Preface

Sathya's Introduction:

This book is the fulfillment of one of my childhood dreams. I wrote my first short story when I was in the 2nd grade—a funny tale, spanning 3-4 pages, complete with a drawing of a car. That story was likely inspired by the movies of M.G. Ramachandran, the former Chief Minister of Tamil Nadu, whose films seemed to be on TV every time we turned it on. My next venture into storytelling came in the 8th grade, with a fictional short story titled "Lola Lible's Castle," inspired by J.K. Rowling's *Harry Potter* series. Then my school friends made an attempt to write a short story based on a travelogue to Andaman Islands in 9th standard. It was an imaginary story written with childhood joy and naivety. Unfortunately, one of our friends lost the manuscript book. Few days later, a surprisingly similar story was published in the children's comic book. That was a shock for us and we all felt sad. Storytelling has always been a part of me, and now, it has taken the shape of this book. In this book I share my life journey. I hope readers can learn from my mistakes and the motley experiences of my life.

I hail from Madurai, a city lovingly known as the Temple City in Tamil Nadu, South India. Now I live in Berlin, Germany in 2022. This book chronicles my journey from Madurai to Berlin, covering my childhood experiences in Madurai's schools, my engineering days in Madurai, my work experiences in Bangalore, Noida, Gurgaon, my journey into motherhood, and my exploration of a new culture in Germany.

The reason I share my story is that it can be a small spark for people like me coming from a small town with bigger aspirations in their life. It can be for someone who likes to know some of the workings and landscape of the software field. It can be for someone who likes to migrate from India to Germany. I hope this book might inspire girls and boys who want to achieve what they set out to achieve.

There may be a little girl or a boy from a small town who dreams of spreading their wings and flying to another city or country for themselves and their family. I dedicate this book to all the little girls out there with dreams—to strive, to grow, and to succeed.

Also this book is not only my story. My husband has also shared his story. We have weaved both our life stories into one book. Now over to his introduction.

Nambirajan's introduction:

This book started as a set of morning pages for me. After having read 'Artist's Way' by Julia Cameron, I started writing three pages of A4 sheets every morning. This habit started in around January 2023 and since then I have written three pages almost every weekday morning for more than a year now. What started as writing by longhand on a sheet of paper slowly migrated to typing on the laptop. Initially I missed the physicality of writing with pen and paper but slowly this e-version took over. And of course there have been many days when I have missed writing this morning journal - days when I have been lazy, travel days and more such. But the habit has largely stayed with me.

Initially these morning pages were just random, stream-of-consciousness kind of jotting down. But slowly over months, it became a place for reflection, creation of youtube scripts and for planning as well. I should thank Julia Cameron again for making my mornings a little more soulful, engaged and productive.

While writing these morning pages, my wife got curious about it and asked how about writing a book about our own lives and slowly but surely the idea of this book came into being. And after a few morning pages and of course some afternoon edits and evening revisions, you have this book in your hand. Thanks to my wife for encouraging me to write and complete this book. Without her, this book probably wouldn't have existed and you, dear reader, might not be reading it now. I would have been happy with journals for my own creative pursuits.

My aim with writing this book is to share my life story. My journey from a humble town in Southern Tamil Nadu (Tirunelveli) to a bustling city in the heart of Europe - Berlin. This journey has its own moments of joy, despair, trauma and happiness.

I have written about some of these moments in this book. I believe these stories from our lives serve as stories that inform, educate and move people.

Also it's my first book to have been published. So that's a little W for being a writer, a little Yay to self expression.

Acknowledgments

Sathya:

This book would not be possible without the discipline in writing for past few months. I thank Nambi for numerous brain-storming sessions, helping me to organize the information and to shape this book. I would also thank the inner child within me for holding the passion long enough to complete the book.

I would also like to thank my parents for providing all the opportunities they can to bring me up and also my school teachers, professors, friends mentors from my work force who shaped me up as a better individual in every decisions I made.

Special thanks to the city of Berlin which enabled me to reflect, think, curate and create our first book.

Nambirajan:

Writing a book is a collaborative process. And this book is even more so. I thank my wife for encouraging me to complete this book. I would also like to thanks two AI tools - Claude and ChatGPT which helped in making the sentences better.

I would also like to thank my parents without whom I won't be here now. I am grateful for my parents for their unwavering love and sacrifices and the value they instilled in me. It is the foundations that they laid which enable me to build the homes of my life. I am thankful to my brother who has been supportive in various stages of my life.

Special thanks to Landmark organization which over various points in time provided that ray of hope that shattered the shackles of the past and enabled me to be free and find my own self expression.

Thanks to Sumithra, Williams, Deva, Anna, Berty and Meenu for reading the early drafts of this book and providing feedback. Thanks to Vidhya Hariharan and Raghav Sharma for helping us to shape the book cover. Thanks to my friend Yousuf for providing valuable insights about the book publishing process and helping me to refine the book.

Introduction

How to read this book:

There are 10 chapters in this book with both of us writing our story under each chapter. Within each chapter you will see separate sections for Sathya and Nambirajan where we tell our own story about the chapter. We did this segmentation so you get two different perspectives - a sense of how two different people who grew up in two different places looked at life and then how they studied, worked and got married and continued our journey. The chapters, except for a few, are mostly linear which follow our life story from our early days of childhood till around November 2024.

1

Southern Roots - Growing up in Tamil Nadu

Sathya: *So what is home for you?*

Nambirajan: *Home as defined by Oxford English Dictionary is... 'the place where one lives permanently, especially as a member of a family or household'*

Sathya: *No, I meant what is Home *for you*. What was 'home' during your childhood days since our reader is going to read about our childhood days in this chapter. So it would be better if we can give them a short trailer about this home from childhood days?*

Nambirajan: *Ah, got it. Home for me was where I grew up in my childhood, where I returned to after school. Home was where I spent most of my childhood summer holidays, where I had friends and fun. Home was Tirunelveli and I played and fought with my brother and of course some cricket, some movies too.*

Sathya: *Same for me. Home was where my mother made those* *delicious home food for me. Lots of fighting with my sister and some studying too*

Nambirajan: *Home is not just all nice stuff though. Home has its own dark pages, trauma days and challenges. At one point in our childhood we moved homes within Tirunelveli.*

Sathya: *For me, my grandparents' home was a favorite place of respite from my parents home. But more on that in the chapter.*

Nambirajan: *So how was growing up in a city like Madurai?*

Sathya: *Madurai wasn't really a big city. My memories of Madurai are filled with...*

Nambirajan: *Hold on, that's a cue to the first chapter. Let's begin.*

Sathya - My School Life in Madurai

My memories of Madurai are filled with spending my childhood days at my grandmother's home on the banks of the Vaigai River. It is a beautiful community that's like a scenic village in my memory. For a few years, I was the only child, as my sister Dhivya was born after 4 years. My parents used to live in the city part of Madurai, which I hated a lot. I did not have much to do at their home since I felt lonely there. Whereas my grandparents' home was fun because there were quite a few kids in the neighborhood and their community was thriving. Though it had fewer facilities compared to the city home, my grandparents' home in the village-like side of Madurai was more interesting for me as a child.

I used to love this 'village part' of Madurai. Called *'Mathichiyam'*, it was situated on the banks of the Vaigai River. There were days I would not return to my parents' city home even for 10 days. My first school was located in *Mathichiyam* where I don't remember much of what I studied. But I remember playing a lot in the school and in the home neighborhood.

I had enormous care over there as there was no bias between families. All were living in huts and all kids would play together in the open area in front of huts with cows and stones. We sometimes went to the Vaigai River bank to make cow dung cakes on the rocks, which would be used for running the kitchen stove. All the families slept outside the huts staring at the night sky with stars. I could have food from any of the neighbors' homes and everyone loved me. Whenever I visit that place, it is always joyful during Diwali, Pongal, and all my celebrations never start without visiting them.

Mathichiyam is also the place where Lord Alagar comes every year to give darshan to all the people. This is celebrated as the *'Chithirai Thiruvila'*, a festival celebrated in the Tamil month of Chithirai (typically falls between mid-April and mid-May in the Gregorian calendar). I remember those nights in which they did theatrical plays where stories of 10 avatars of Lord Vishnu were performed the whole night. This ritual continues in Madurai today. Later, my father moved our home to Anna Nagar, which was further away from my grandparents' home in Mathichiyam. With that shift, my visit to my grandparents' home gradually decreased. I guess my father made the move to make us get out of this village life which I enjoyed. Be it the village part of Madurai or the slightly urbanised areas of Madurai, my childhood was firmly within the city of Madurai.

To people who are uninitiated about Madurai, it is a city in Southern India. It is the third-biggest city in Tamil Nadu by population. It is a city which is steeped in Tamil history and culture. As a child, I took its significance for granted. It wasn't until my teenage years, when I delved into books like the *Thirukkural*, that I began to truly appreciate Madurai's rich heritage. Madurai is also the capital of the Pandya kingdom, one of the three major Tamil empires in Southern India. The city has witnessed various epochs, starting with the first Tamil Sangam for Tamil literature, which is believed to have lasted from 9600 BC to 5200 BC. Madurai is also associated with '*Kannagi*' the legendary heroine of the Tamil literature epic '*Silapathikram*'. The magnificent Madurai Meenakshi Amman Temple, constructed by the Pandya dynasty between the 12th and 14th centuries, and later expanded by King Tirumala Nayak in the 16th century, stands as a testament to its glorious past. Yet, despite living there for nearly 16 years, my visits to the Meenakshi Amman Temple were few and far between.

Madurai has also played a significant role in India's pre-independence movement. In 1921, Mahatma Gandhi made the revolutionary decision in Madurai to boycott Western attire and embrace the dhoti, a symbol of Indian identity. The city is also the birthplace of Bharatanatyam dancer and the founder of Kalakshetra, Mrs. Rukmini Devi Arundale. Many illustrious figures such as Carnatic singer M.S. Subbulakshmi, and Google CEO Sundar Pichai hail from here. Today, Madurai is known for its warm-hearted people and its culinary delights, especially non-vegetarian dishes like 'kari dosa'. The city has also inspired Tamil movies like *'Paruthi Veeran'* which got critical and popular acclaim. A recent example is 'Kottukaali'. It was screened at this year's Berlinale International Film Festival and is set in Madurai.

Madurai has changed drastically over the years. In the 1990s, it was a peaceful, less commercialized city with minimal traffic. My sister and I used to play on the quiet streets, untroubled by large vehicles. By the 2000s, Madurai had modernized with shopping malls, cinemas, and more vehicles on the roads. When I visited in 2023, I found a fast-paced city where even auto drivers and fruit sellers used digital applications like PhonePe and Ola. We can take Ola cabs and autos, but the habit of charging extra on top of the basic fare has not gone. However, I missed the slower, more leisurely Madurai of my childhood.

Enough about the city; let me share the story of my early days in Madurai. Coming from a middle-class family, my mother Shanthi was a housewife, and my father Balakrishnan was the sole breadwinner. He was the first graduate in his family, among nine siblings, and was determined to provide a good education for my sister Dhivya and me, despite the high cost of education in India.

As a child, I was playful and had a strong aversion to mathematics, despite my father's B.Sc. degree in the subject. My father used to come a little early during my preparation for math exams and helped me with understanding the match concepts.

Most days I used to go with tears for my Maths exam. He would lose his patience when I did wrong calculations, and I had a tough time with math and my father. I prayed when the exam timetable was published. I always wished Maths would be the last exam in the timetable, so that I can forget about it and enjoy a joyful summer holiday. I was very happy when I got a pass mark in Maths, but my father was worried. Until the third grade, I got more interested in playing than studying.

My parents wanted to make me get serious about my studies in the early years of schooling. One way they did this was by sending me for tuition. I should thank them for this decision as my tuition teachers like Mrs. Minakshi, Mrs. Latha made the concepts and fundamentals clear for me. I attended Fusco's Convent, a Catholic school known for its discipline, until the eighth grade. From 3rd grade onwards, my father's worry disappeared as I started scoring good marks and being among the top 3 rank holders of the class. Now I can understand that a little more attention in any aspect of life makes a huge difference.

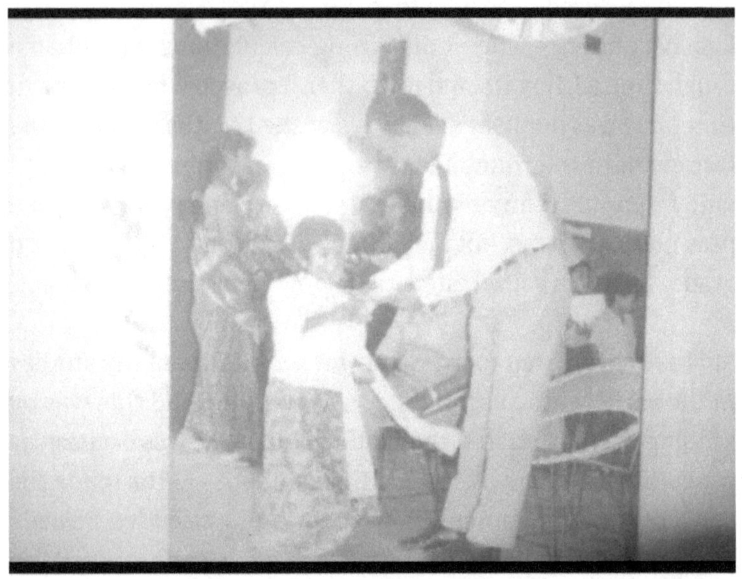

Me receiving the grand prize for winning lemon and school competition in Fusco's convent

Fusco's Convent is also the place where I first discovered my passion for public speaking. This school holds a special place in my heart. My English teacher, Latha, who also tutored me, encouraged me to participate in an elocution competition in the third grade. She gave me a write-up on 'Transportation' to memorize. Despite my nervousness and trembling legs, I managed to complete my speech and earned third place, just as my teacher had predicted. This experience gradually reduced my fears and sparked my interest in other forms of creative expression. Teachers like Mrs. Latha and Mrs. Meenakshi played vital roles in helping me with my speech scripts. Through these creative competitions, I discovered my love for public speaking and engaging with an audience. I remember my mother getting emotional when I spoke on stage in front of a crowd. That incident once made me stumble with my next lines. From then on, whenever I spoke on stage, I kept my eye contact far away from the known circle of people in the audience.

Another funny incident that happened during my studies at Fusco's school. I always admired the 'Art from Waste' displays at Fuscos School, eagerly exploring the creations that occupied both floors in the school. One year, a senior crafted a stunning penguin entirely from eggshells, which left me in awe. Inspired, I decided to replicate it for the next year's Fine Arts competition. When my own eggshell penguin was displayed, my juniors were impressed.

My sister Dhivya, in first grade, shared the story of my creation with her friend Moni, who loved it and wanted to buy it. I quoted ten rupees, and Moni managed to bring the money the next day. I felt thrilled, thinking I had a budding business. But things took a funny turn when Moni's mother called, upset after mistakenly thinking she had bought broken eggshells. My mother, trying to suppress her laughter, advised us to stick to art and leave business out of school. That became a funny and memorable story from our school days.

A pivotal moment in my school life was being nominated for inter-school *Thirukkural* competitions. The *Thirukkural* is a classic Tamil Sangam literature consisting of 1,330 couplets, each dealing with everyday virtues. Participants had to recite

60-100 verses along with their meanings. Initially, I disliked these competitions due to the complex verses, but I eventually became a regular participant. One of my favorite couplets is:

"Thottanaith thoorum manarkeni maandharkku
Katranaith thoorum arivu,"

which translates to: 'Water will flow from a well in the sand in proportion to the depth to which it is dug; knowledge will flow from a man in proportion to his learning.'

The *Thirukkural* significantly shaped my character during childhood and fueled my joy for public speaking at Fusco's Convent. It is also the school where I had moral science classes. The teacher of this subjective class shared stories from the Bible and also other stories compiled in the moral science book. They took immense responsibility in shaping the students with morals values.

In the 8th grade, my family had to shift our home as my father was constructing a house with his entire savings. We moved from a one-bedroom rented home to a larger, more spacious house. However, the new house was far from Fusco's Convent, so we had to change schools. I felt bad to leave this school where my childhood and pre-teen years had been shaped. It was hard for me to leave my street and school friends behind. I had a few friends like Yazhisai, Saranya, Paul, Raja Rajan, and Siva Shankari. All these friends were either my tuition cum school friends or my friends who participated along with me in competitions like debate, quiz, Rangoli and so on. I can't forget those choir days, setting up the microphone every day in the stadium for prayer. I happily enjoyed those activities in our school. As we had to move on to a new home, we moved to another school with hope in the 9th standard. That's when we discovered Krishnammal Ramasubbaiyer School (KRMS), located near Madurai Airport. KRMS is managed by '*Dinamalar*', a popular Tamil newspaper company in Madurai. Although the school was still quite a distance from our new home, the bus facilities made it manageable to get to the school.

Transferring to KRMS in the ninth grade was a revelation. The compassion and care at this school were remarkable. KRMS played a massive role in developing my public speaking skills. Teachers like Mrs. Indra, Mrs. Subhu Lakshmi, Mrs. Shanthi, and Mrs. Devyani taught Mathematics, Biology, History, and Physics in such an engaging manner that learning became super enjoyable. My time at KRMS was the golden period of my school life. I even received a gold ring from my mathematics teacher, Mrs. Indra, for scoring a centum (100/100) in mathematics on my board exam.

KRMS had a unique model where students and teachers stayed in the school hostel for six months to better focus on preparing for the 10th standard board exams. The hostel food was delicious and healthy, and the campus was surrounded by nature, which likely sparked my love for plants. We would find only a thin line separating the classroom and nature. The school's comprehensive approach, including quizzes, multiple-choice questions, and long-answer writing sessions, ensured thorough preparation. I also appreciated the school's empathetic environment. I felt comfortable discussing sensitive topics, like my fears about menstruation. During an evening study session, I had a menstrual mishap that stained the chair. While a nearby student reacted with alarm, my biology teacher calmly explained that it was a normal biological phenomenon and nothing to be ashamed of. She even advised me to maintain a healthy iron-rich diet for period stability.

This supportive environment at KRMS helped me and my classmates excel—after our 10th-grade board exams, all nine students in our class scored meritoriously, and I secured the top rank in the school, with my name proudly displayed on the school notice board. My sincere thanks to school founder Mr. Ramasubbu for imagining and creating such a wonderful educational space in Madurai. He used to visit our class and motivate us before our board exams and, in fact, arranged a short trip for us to feel a little more relaxed before the board exams. They always believed in 'Quality rather than Quantity'. Class strength never crossed more than 20 students, and they used to provide us a cup of hot milk during our recess time to feel more refreshed. Those were the breezy, happy memorable days of KRMS.

After completing my 10th standard, we began looking for good higher secondary schools. I enrolled in St. Joseph's Convent for the 11th standard. St. Joseph's was a super-crowded girls' school, and I felt lost in the sea of students. Unlike KRMS, where teachers knew every student, only the brightest students were recognized here. I struggled to fit in, often feeling isolated due to my conservative dress and large *pottu/ bindi (*a decorative mark, usually a dot, worn on the forehead, symbolizing cultural, spiritual, or aesthetic significance, particularly in South Asian traditions)

Determined to make my mark, I participated in the 'Turn-a-Coat' competition during a fine arts event. The challenge was to speak for two minutes in favor of a topic and then switch to speaking against it for the next two minutes. The topic I was assigned was 'Hitler.' At that young age, unaware of the full extent of his atrocities, I initially spoke positively about him, viewing him through the limited lens of Indian historical education. However, my later visits to the Holocaust Memorial and concentration camps in Berlin profoundly changed my perspective. I realized the monstrous acts committed by Hitler which killed millions of people. These experiences revealed the gravity of his crimes and the enduring impact of his actions.

In India, some people still regard Hitler as a role model, a view shaped by a narrow understanding of history. However, in Germany, the word 'Hitler' is not allowed in public spaces due to the immense sensitivity around his legacy. Personally, I believe the true leader who contributed significantly to Germany's progress is Angela Merkel. Her leadership brought about remarkable improvements in various sectors, and she remains an inspiring figure for me.

Reflecting on the competitions I participated in school, it became a pivotal moment that, along with my academic performance, earned me recognition from both teachers and students at St. Joseph's. Time flew by, and I excelled in my board exams, especially in biology, where I topped the subject for the entire school in 2006. My time at St. Joseph's was made even more memorable by two close friends, Subha and Bala, who brought fun and joy to my school life.

I always dreamed of becoming a genetic engineer, while most of my classmates aspired to be doctors. I learned about advanced genetic engineering programs in Germany, such as those at the Max Planck Research Institute. However, my father insisted I pursue computer science engineering to ensure financial independence—a common aspiration for middle-class families at the time. Despite my interest in biotechnology, I ended up enrolling in a private engineering college in Madurai for a computer science course. Computer science promised quicker job opportunities, especially as cities like Bangalore and Chennai were emerging as software hubs in India.

Though my dream of becoming a genetic engineer remained unfulfilled, my journey to Germany eventually became a reality. This book chronicles some of that journey, highlighting the challenges and triumphs along the way.

Nambirajan - Growing up in Tirunelveli

Tirunelveli is a city in the southern part of Tamil Nadu which in itself is in the southern part of India. So it's fair to say I come from the deep south of India. Tirunelveli is known for its halwa which was created many years back by a king who got a Rajasthani halwai to make some halwas for him. The name Tirunelveli itself has a story in it. The myth is that there was once a farmer who had kept some *nel* (rice paddy) to dry and gone about his work. Then it started raining. Since the *nel* has to be kept dry, the farmer prays to Lord Shiva to keep his crops dry. He returns to his crop and by some magic, his crops remain dry while the whole surrounding area has become wet due to the rains. Since the god became a fence (*veli* in Tamil) to the paddy crops, the place is known as Tiru-nel-veli (the god who stood as a fence to the paddy crops). There is Nellaiyappar temple which is also a popular religious temple in Tirunelveli..

I spent my entire school life in one place—St. Francis Xavier Matric Higher Secondary School in Tirunelveli. Yes, from kindergarden to 12th grade, for about 14 years, it was the same school, the same uniform, and often the same set of friends. There are pros and cons to such consistency. On the one hand, you grow up with the same people and evolve with them. Also studying in the same institution provides you with an anchor which is useful especially when the other major institution in your life i.e. Home become shaky (which it did for a few years). On the other hand, there's no mystery, no sudden changes in scenery or fresh starts to keep things interesting.

I was an average student till about class 6 and then slowly I became good at studies. My academic career peaked in 10th grade and after that it was all downhill from there. I was interested in English and loved to read stories in my non detailed subject. I still remember reading Scarlet Pimpernel and about Sherlock Holmes solving murders in Arthur Conan Doyle's 'Hound of the Baskervilles' much before the chapters were introduced in the classroom by our English teacher. Looking back retrospectively, I could have chosen a B.A./ M.A. in English literature to further my interest in English language. But coming from a middle-class family, I had only two options - Doctor or an Engineer. And being the second kid whose elder brother had already gone to an Engineering college, I had only one option - to be a doctor.

What they say is true - students in Tamil Nadu (and to a larger extent India) do Engineering and then they figure out what they want to do in life. But I am getting ahead of myself here. Let me come back to this Hobson's choice later.

Let me share something about my family. My father worked as an 'Assistant Manager' in 'Aavin', a Tamil Nadu based government organization in India that produces and distributes dairy products like milk, curd, ghee, butter and more. One of the perks of working in Aavin is that he gets a packet of the sweet 'Aavin palkova' during Diwali time, which I remember tasting during my childhood days. My mother worked as a Health Supervisor in a primary health care center in Tirunelveli. Both worked in the same firm till about their retirement age. My grandfather from my father's side is from agrarian background and lived in Nagalkulam. My grandfather from my mother's side worked in the local court in Tirunelveli as a administrative official.

I had an elder brother who was my primary nemesis for the first 15 years of my life. There have been many a fight between him and me for something as trivial as who has gotten more '*muttai poriyal*' (Tamil version of scrambled eggs) or about who gets the first dosai (a rice batter-based crepe like dish). My brother and I would also fight for '*Siruvar Malar*' - a Friday supplemental magazine for children that came with Dinamalar magazine - every Friday to the point of sometimes pulling it out from both ends and tearing it. My mother came up with the brilliant idea that they could have just got two newspapers on Friday. This was many years after we were fighting and losing our morning sleep for the children's magazine.

My family pic circa 1988. I am the youngest one beside my mother sitting on a wooden barrel

Talking about my nemesis, I need to talk about my friends too. I had a few friends in school and on my street. One of my best friends who traveled with me almost my entire school life (and some more) was Nirmal, who now works as an Orthopedic doctor in Tirunelveli. Rajesh was another school friend who shared the same birthday as me. Rashik was my first quiz partner (we botched our first quiz though). There was Nawaz and his younger brother (with whom we used to play cricket), my Super Mario video game friends, my ground cricket friends and more. I might have forgotten their names but some of their memories are still alive.

One such memory was with Bala Murugan and Bala Krishnan,

brothers who stayed near our home. I remember going to their home and making drawings where we would cut out shapes from newspapers and use a toothbrush dipped in ink to spray the outlines. Those were fun summer days. The Bala brothers were also the people to introduce us to the Super Mario video game which we later bought for ourselves. For a few summers, we spent countless hours helping Mario rescue the princess and I was one of the local champions in our street who could complete all the 8×4 levels in one sitting. Super Mario Bros. still continues to be one of my favorite games. Between playing Mario, playing street cricket (the national game for all boys in India) and watching some *Shaktiman* series on TV, most of our childhood was spent.

Another memory that's still fresh in my mind was about academic competitions. There was one which I won and another which I failed. First was an essay writing competition in Tamil for which we sought help from a Tamil teacher near our home. He wrote an essay with flowery words and rhyming sentences in Tamil which I promptly mugged up and then wrote that in the competition. I remember winning some prizes for it.

My brother and I (in my favorite Orange t shirt)

Then there was a Tamil elocution – which still gives me haunting memories. Being a super shy kid, I wasn't aware of the theatrics needed to win a Tamil elocution. This elocution was organized at *Aryaas*, a hotel near my home, and we went there to see a room packed with kids. Though I had my material memorized, I wasn't speaking it so loud and clear. A kid who went before me was almost jumping up and down and gave his speech with full theatrics and animation (which is what judges in those days, and still typically, reward). I went and, in my normal mode, gave my speech. Needless to say, I lost, and the theatrical kid won. My mother was disappointed that I wasn't as theatrical as the other kid.

What I was good at, though, was quizzing. During my school days, we had a chemistry teacher, **Jebaraj sir**, who also doubled up as a General Knowledge (GK) teacher. What he used to do was complete the syllabus in a few weeks and then use the rest of the GK periods to conduct quizzes in the class. He would split the class into two sections to conduct a mini quiz within the classroom. I still remember being excited for the General Knowledge period and answering the questions, which he would typically ask from recent current affairs and world events. More often than not, our team would win these mini quizzes. In a bid to prepare myself to win these quizzes, I started reading *The Hindu* newspaper, most of whose content went above my head. Still, I read what I could and prepared for the quizzes. I wanted to read books outside of my syllabus to learn and be prepared for such G.K. quizzes. But my parents weren't very supportive of buying books that weren't part of the syllabus. All they wanted from me was to study well in school subjects and score more marks.

Another quiz we missed attending during our school days was *The Hindu's* Young World Quiz. The closest center to us was Madurai, and having a quiz of that caliber was like a once-in-a-blue-moon event. As fate would have it, we also had some other competition in another school on the same day. After much thinking, my quiz mate *Rashik* and I decided to go to the smaller quiz and win the prize rather than go to the bigger competition of the Young World Quiz in Madurai and lose there. And, as luck would have it, we lost the small school quiz too, which meant it was a double whammy for us – we missed the Young World quiz and lost the other quiz too. There was a lesson right there for me: when you have an opportunity to go to a bigger ground and take on a bigger game, do that no matter the win or lose. There is a *Thirukural* about this, which conveys this better:

'Kaana Muyaleydha Ampinil Yaanai
  Pizhaiththavel Endhal Inidhu'

Which means it's better to aim at a big elephant and fail rather than to aim at a rabbit and succeed. What's an aspect of your lives, dear reader, where you are happy with aiming at the small rabbit? Most of us, at different times in our lives, choose to go for the small rabbit and be happy with it. Enough of my Deepak Chopra mode, back to my life.

But quizzes like these were few and far between. Most of my school life was about studies, studies, studies, and marks, marks, and marks. I took math tuition, which helped me get a good grasp of my numbers, and chemistry tuition, which improved my chemistry with that subject. All of these, combined with enough support from my dad and my mother, helped me get 3 'centums' – 100 marks – in Science and Math in my board exams. I also managed to breach the 1000 mark, scoring an impressive 1006 out of a possible 1100. Only three other students managed to do that in my class, and all three were girls. So, you can say I was the only boy superstar in my class when it came to academics. It couldn't get better academically, and I was basking in glory for a month or so after my tenth board exams.

When it comes to academics, my learning curve for my academic life looks something like this:

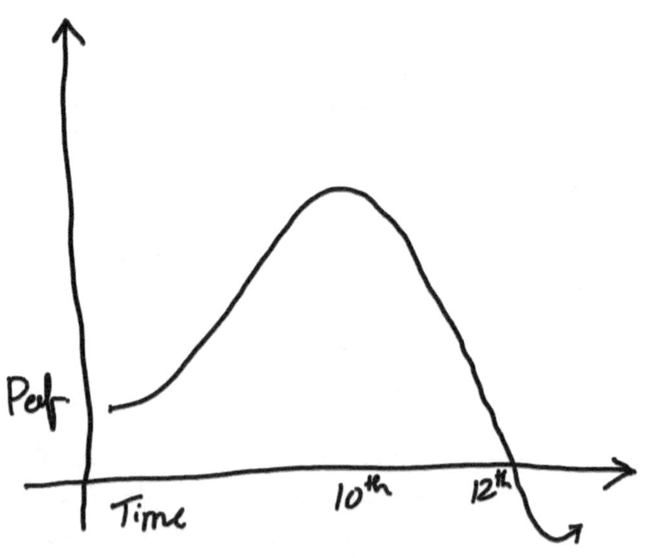

My academic performance vs Time – Scale complete accurate to the nearest pixel

After having scored highly in my tenth and being featured in a newspaper ad by my school, I became the '*NAMBIkkai natchathiram*' (promising star?) of my family. They hoped that I would get even higher marks in 12th grade and get qualified to study medicine and become a doctor for my career. But my academic career started floundering in 11th, and in 12th grades, it went south even further.

The next big exam was the 12th standard board exams. In those days, we had entrance exams, and they would combine the board theory marks with the entrance exam marks to form the cutoff marks. Though I did put in good efforts in my 12th grade as well, things didn't turn out as well or click just as right as they did in my 10th grade. I also made a few mistakes. I became a fan of a particular biriyani from a roadside shop, which I later learned was beef biriyani. I would gorge on it to the point of having three biriyanis on the same day. This led to me being overweight and losing some of my intellectual sharpness. Also, my brother was no longer at home, having left for Coimbatore to pursue engineering at PSG College of Engineering. With no nemesis at home, I also lost my competitive spirit a bit. Tuitions became too much of a stressful thing, and the pressure of the 12th grade board exams also added up. All of this meant a below-par performance from me in the final exams.

I scored only 1126/1200 in my final 12th grade board exams, and my medical cutoff was 285/300. Not bad for an average student – that's a 93% score. But not for me – a rising star in my 10th standard. Also, the medical cutoff was not enough to secure an MBBS seat in one of the government medical colleges like MMC (Madras Medical College), SMC (Stanley Medical College), or even TMC (Tirunelveli Medical College). I needed something like 296+ to safely secure a seat in a government medical college in Tamil Nadu. Bottom line: I am not going to be a doctor with these marks.

Two years prior, my elder brother had gotten lesser marks than me in his 12th grade. But there was no pressure or expectation on him, and he chose engineering at PSG Engineering College in Coimbatore. Now that he had chosen engineering, I 'had to' be a doctor – which meant extra expectations and extra pressure for me. And now that I had fewer marks for a medical seat, my father came up with a 'clever' idea – to have me join in improvement. Improvement, in theory, is basically for those kids who had to miss board exams or couldn't prepare properly because of some unfortunate incidents. But over the years, it became like a backdoor entry for getting a medical seat, where thousands of kids would appear for theory and entrance exams again to improve their marks and make an attempt at getting a medical seat. Though I went to Thiyagaraja College for the placements in my first attempt for 12th grade exams, my father refused to pay and pick any engineering seat. Now I had to come back and do improvement. I remember crying and feeling sad all the way from Madurai to Tirunelveli in a bus. My friends and peers would join engineering colleges. Meanwhile, I would have to redo 12th to improve my marks. I felt like I was missing moving onto the next chapter of my life. Though I was not for improvement, my parents cajoled and goaded me to do it again. And thus began my year of improvement, which I will share in detail later in a chapter of traumas – a fitting place for a year of studies and reappearing for exams.

Coming back to our school, one of the other great teachers I had was **Mangai sir.** I started studying chemistry tuition with him for my tenth standard. Chemistry was a subject I'd always struggled with, so my parents enrolled me in a tuition class with Mangai Manavalan, the superstar of chemistry teachers in Tirunelveli. A few of my friends – *Natrajan*, *Gopi*, *Siva*, *Anantha* – and I would take the bus to Maharaja Nagar every evening for those classes. In December of the 10th standard, Mangai Sir took off for a month for a long work trip to Chennai, and instead of missing the classes, sitting at home and studying, we didn't inform our parents and still went to the classes during those days as if the classes were there. We used that time to goof off in a nearby park. It was like the universe had gifted us a month of carefree fun right before the grind of exam prep began. Then he became our school teacher for chemistry in the 11th and 12th standard.

Another remarkable teacher is **Johnson sir**, who taught us English. I still remember him spending countless hours teaching English grammar, which I hated, and breezing through non-detail and prose chapters, which I liked. There was once a discussion in our class on a poem called 'Lines Composed Upon Westminster Bridge' by William Wordsworth, which has these lines:

'In his first splendor, valley, rock, or hill;
Ne'er saw I, never felt, a calm so deep!
The river glideth at his own sweet will:
Dear God! the very houses seem asleep;
And all that mighty heart is lying still!'

After reading this line, I raised my hand and asked a question: "Usually rivers are mentioned in feminine form, but Wordsworth says the Thames river as 'his will' and not 'her will'. Why is it so?" Though he answered it in some way, I wasn't satisfied with his answer. But thanks to him for being open and kindling our curiosity in English literature. Reading Alfred Lord Tennyson's poems, learning about 'Two roads diverged in a yellow wood' were some of my favorite memories of learning English from my school days.

Looking back at my school life, St. Francis Xavier wasn't just my school—it was a constant in my life during a time when everything else seemed to be in flux. My family was going through a tough period, moving houses frequently due to a legal battle involving my father and a tenant. Yet, through it all, my school stood firm, growing alongside me. When I started, the classrooms were practically huts; by the time I left, they were solid concrete buildings. The school went from being an unknown entity to a well-known brand in the city. But more than the buildings, it's the connect with the people there—that formed the other major bedrock in my childhood life. That which carried me through the troughs when my family issues got a bit volatile.

Retrospectively looking at my school life, there were a few lessons. Like I said before, 10th grade was the pinnacle of my academic life, where I managed to score a perfect 100 in Maths, Chemistry, and Physics. I even made it into the school's newspaper ad, which showcased the top four students. That year, everything just clicked. The high scores also brought another reward—which is that my school waived off the entire academic tuition fee for my 11th and 12th grades. This came at a time when we were debating whether to have me join a new school like Jayendra, another reputed school in Tirunelveli. But the fee waiver effectively made us drop all those plans. Probably, I could have benefited from a new school and a new set of friends. Maybe being with a bigger group of students would have brought out some more competitive spirit in me, which was lagging in my school towards the end of my school studies.

A lesson I learnt from my childhood is the power of consistency: I had morning tuition for Maths, and though I can't recall much from those classes, I do remember my dad waking up early to drop me off at 6 a.m. A year of consistent effort in both Maths and Chemistry paid off with those perfect scores. Maybe that's one way to achieve what you set out to do—just the right amount of effort without going overboard.

So, that's a snapshot of my school days. A kid who peaked in 10th grade, stumbled in 12th grade. There are plenty more stories to tell, from my 'Improvement days' and especially from some of the traumas of my childhood, but let's save those for a chapter titled 'Joyful Recollections of Trauma.' Trust me, that will be an interesting read. For now though, you have to first get through one of Sathya's boring monologues about her college days.

2

Campus Chronicles - Our College Life

Sathya: *So college is when childhood Home becomes what you want to move away from?*

Nambirajan: *Yes, many want the freedom that comes with staying away from your parents. Home becomes where you stay with friends/ classmates. Also it's a place where you maybe, sometimes study for your college subjects?*

Sathya: *Coming to college, did you pick the course which you wanted? I couldn't pick the course which I wanted. My father made me pick something different.*

Nambirajan: *That's the same for me. In fact it's the same for many kids in India. Parents living their life through the kids. Also I was clueless what i wanted for sometime and had to make mistakes to learn*

Sathya: *Making mistakes is essential part of your growing up early days*

Nambirajan: *yes but when you were actually making mistakes it wasn't fun*

Sathya: *Talking of fun, what was your most fun experience in college?*

Nambirajan: *That would be attending KBC experience. For a small town kid to get to go to a big city like Mumbai and play the game show with Shahrukh as host you had been dreaming about. What was your most fun moment in college?*

Sathya: *Being with my friend Subha was the most fun. I couldn't remember much else. I was in the same city, Madurai doing a course...*

Nambirajan: *Hold on. Probably you can continue that in the chapter?*

Sathya - From Biotech to Computer Science

I made peace with my father's choice of a software engineering course and began my studies as a day scholar in 2006 at K.L.N. College of Engineering. This college was located in my hometown of Madurai. It was started in the 1990s by and for the Saurashtrian community, which had significant number of people living in Madurai. Initially, my preferred choice was Biotechnology. If I had pursued that at the Coimbatore Institute of Technology, I would have explored a new city and perhaps found more experienced mentors. Coimbatore, like Chennai, is known for its reputed educational institutions in Tamil Nadu. In contrast, I assumed that a smaller city like Madurai would have more judgments and comparisons in everything and anything. However, I eventually generated my interest from within and trained my mind to like this college during the first year. My major goal was to secure a job before completing my final year and move out of Madurai. I did not care to have friends in college, as the college where I studied was selected out of compulsion. As time passed by, I had acquaintances who later became friends, like Yatra, Dhivaharan, and Vivek (some names changed to protect privacy). In higher secondary schools and colleges, we would start seeing groups formed in our class, and they tend to remain as friends. I somehow did not fit into this concept, and so I liked to be a little alone, but still being acquainted with these groups.

Engineering degree course span four years. During the first three years, I traveled extensively for paper presentation competitions. These paper presentations were not as research-intensive as those conducted by doctorate scholars, but they allowed us to do small-scale research on topics of interest and present our understanding, helping us improve our presentation skills.

In my third year, I remember traveling to Bhabha Atomic Research Centre (BARC) in Mumbai, as my essay on Electron Beam Technology had been selected in an All India Essay writing competition. This was my first travel experience outside Tamil Nadu. Having never traveled beyond Madurai, I was unfamiliar with bus or rail routes. This trip was an eye-opener for me in many ways. I learned to travel alone and understood my strengths and weaknesses. I spent 10 days at the BARC (Bhabha Atomic Research Center) campus with fellow participants from different colleges across India, mainly interacting with physics students as the program was heavily focused on physics. BARC was founded by Homi J Bhabha, a pioneer of the Indian Nuclear program.

BARC, located in Anushakti Nagar at Mumbai, is a vast community with its own schools, colleges, cafeterias, parks, and apartments for its employees and their families. This experience made me appreciate Homi J. Bhabha's contributions to nuclear research and science in India. At BARC, I participated in a guided tour of nuclear reactors, Electron Beam Technology plants, Tarapur Power Station, Tata Cancer Research Institute, and the streets of Anushakti Nagar, creating memorable moments with my fellow participants.

However, I struggled with language barriers. Although I had learned Hindi since the first grade, spoken Hindi was not prevalent in Tamil Nadu, which has a strong aversion to Hindi, much like Germany's aversion to English. This was the first time I truly felt the need for spoken Hindi, especially when trying to communicate with auto drivers and socialize with my fellow participants.

On the ninth day, after visiting all the reactors, we had to present our work on Electron Beam Technology. The jury comprised 4-5 scientists in a large opera-style auditorium. Despite some discouragement from other participants due to my background in computer science, I managed to present with clarity and answer the jury's questions. To my astonishment,

I won 2nd prize in the competition, with a grand ceremony led by Anil Kakodkar, the chairman of BARC, where I received a cash prize of 10,000 rupees—a significant amount at the time. However, the most valuable takeaway was the advice from one of the jury scientists: to be myself, authentic in my thoughts and accent. She emphasized that speaking clear English with simple words is more powerful than trying to adopt a British accent. This experience taught me that effective communication is about being understood, not about adopting a different accent. From then on, I started speaking in simple English without trying to change my accent.

There were also some simple, joyful moments in the trip. We had buffet lunches in every BARC institute, served in porcelain cutlery—a royal treatment for me in those times. During this time, we celebrated Diwali in Mumbai, with fairy lights adorning the streets and apartment balconies, and fresh sweet stalls selling cashews and nuts. Cashews, in particular, were a luxury, and my mother usually reserved them for special sweets like *Paayasam.* These were some of my fond memories from Mumbai.

After the grand ceremony on the 10th day, I had to travel alone from Mumbai to Madurai, a two-day journey. One participant helped me get bus tickets as my train ticket was on the waiting list. He accompanied me until Salem, but the rest of the journey was challenging. I also suffered from a stomach upset, which added to the difficulty. The bus stops lacked good toilets, but I somehow managed to reach Madurai. Reflecting on this journey, I realized the importance of learning native languages that are spoken in the place and safe travel practices. With my prize money, I bought my first Nokia phone, a 3100 model, and spent the remaining 5,000 rupees on a PHP software course, although I soon realized I didn't enjoy the course.

My college celebrated my achievement at BARC by featuring my photo in their newsletter. I owe a lot to my Head of Department, Dr. Lakshmi Narasimhan, an inspiring mentor who encouraged participation in inter-college symposiums and projects. He often shared his experiences from multinational companies, bringing a global perspective into our classrooms. Sadly, we lost him in 2017 when he drowned while trying to save his son during a family vacation at Thirukkurungudi near Tirunelveli, South India. Sadly, both lost their lives in this tragic incident.

My next travel experience was for a paper presentation at BITS Pilani. Knowing my limited proficiency in Hindi, I knew this would be another challenging trip. My friend Yatra and I submitted our paper, and to our excitement, it was selected. We were thrilled to experience BITS Pilani, a benchmark institution in India. My friend Yatra's home was in Delhi, so we booked a 2nd class sleeper train from Madurai to Delhi, a two-day journey that left us sweaty and in dirty clothes.

This was my first time visiting North India, and my expectations of cities like Delhi were shattered. I had imagined North Indian cities to be cleaner with better infrastructure, but Delhi was dirty and dusty, with roads stained by *paan*. Compared to Southern India—states like Tamil Nadu, Kerala, and Karnataka, which are greener and have more comfortable public buses—Delhi was a disappointment. My English did not help much in Delhi, but I learned the word '*bhaiya*' (Hindi word for brother) during our train travel. After a short rest at Yatra's house, Yatra's family driver drove us to BITS Pilani. The route was deserted, as Pilani is near the Thar Desert, with camels and scorching heat.

We arrived at BITS Pilani at 9:30 P.M. and were immediately impressed by the huge campus. The students had a lot of autonomy, with cycles for commuting between departments. BITS students were outspoken and courageous, and the symposium we attended was entirely organized by student volunteers. They even invited Jimmy Wales from Wikipedia as a guest speaker. Although we didn't win the competition, I conquered my fear. That is when I understood the power of courage and to do the work that our heart and mind says.

I spent my college days focusing on projects, presentations, and public speaking, skills that continue to serve me well today. I believe I'm better at demonstrations and engaging listeners, and this remains a key aspect of my work. Despite my success in public speaking, I've always been an introvert with a fear of large crowds. There were times when I fainted in crowded places, and my parents were always anxious about taking me to crowded temples. Although I've worked on this issue, I still struggle with it. I still avoid gatherings and get togethers. I would rather have conversations in one-on-one meetings rather than being part of a big crowd.

Another challenge I faced during my teenage years was my appearance and grooming of my personality. As a shy kid from a conservative background, I didn't pay much attention to my clothing during my teenage years. I used to wear a non-ironed uniform, a big bindi, not being properly combed, and using a hairpin to fix my shawl rather than a pin, which was the norm. Basically, I did not conform to the beauty/grooming standards of that time. I also wore big spectacles and didn't pay much attention to how I carried myself.

This laid-back attitude to grooming and presenting myself resulted in some undesirable outcomes. There weren't many friends for me during my school and college days. There were also some depressing remarks. One day, while visiting a friend's home, her mother asked me what I would want to do in my future. I replied, "I want to do journalism and be a news reader at BBC." She looked at me and said, "You personality is zero." It was a heartbreaking comment, but when I shared this with my school friend Subha, she comforted me and advised me not to pay attention to it. Nevertheless, I worked on improving my appearance with healthy diets rather than a makeover and gradually built more confidence. As a teenager, such comments can undermine your confidence and cause self-doubt, but I slowly began to work on my health, which resulted in a better appearance. I took suggestions from Subha and started to spend more time on my grooming and public speaking. Eventually, the mirror began to reflect a more confident version of myself. It *is* true—when we put more energy into any aspect of our lives, it transforms for the better.

My final year of college was a life-changing phase. I remember my first job interview, which was for a famous telecom company whose name rhymes with Tricent. It was one of the few companies offering a good salary at the time—3.5 Lakhs INR annually. After completing the aptitude test, I eagerly awaited the selection list and was called as the 26th candidate for the next round. I cleared the Group Discussion and moved on to the technical interview the following day. Thanks to advice from my senior Prasanna, who had gone through the process the previous year, I approached the interview with confidence. Although I wasn't particularly passionate about programming, I had a solid grasp of the basics of Data Structures, which is fundamental to programming in operating systems and other complex areas. If you understand Linked Lists, the interview is a breeze. I owe my understanding of Data Structures to Professor Ramesh, who taught the subject with passion. Even after a decade, I remember the flow and logic behind it. During the interview, I was given three sets of problems, which I solved on paper, clearly explaining my logic to the interviewer.

My college batch from KLN Engineering College, Madurai. I am fifth from the left in the sitting row – Sathya

Despite a nagging doubt about whether I would enjoy being a software developer, I was overjoyed to receive the job offer and the opportunity to leave Madurai. For children from middle-class families, getting into college is often about securing a decent job. Achieving that dream job can elevate your life to a new level. My first job empowered me and significantly improved my confidence. My mother, Shanthi, a strong and bold woman, didn't have a bank account or a job. She saved money from what my father gave her to run the household. I remember helping her open her first bank account. Seeing her insecurities due to financial dependence on my father motivated me to grab the opportunity and be on my own feet.

In a couple of months, our entire family met with a fatal accident while returning from Chennai. We had gone to Chennai for my sister Dhivya's college selection meeting. While returning, we met with the accident. It is the darkest chapter of our life. While returning after our lunch, we all slept off, and there were no traces of thought on how the accident happened. We lost our mother a month later due to a severe head injury. Dhivya, my father, and I suffered hand and leg fractures. We lost our driver on the spot of the accident. My dad fell into depression and carries a lot of guilt to this day for opting for the car drive. He became an alcoholic after this incident. When I think about this now, there are a few mistakes that stand out as lessons. Firstly, we should have taken public transport like trains instead of private vehicles. Secondly, never drive after a heavy lunch on the highway. There was huge money spent on treatment by my dad, as we did not have medical insurance. It was an unimaginable expense. I am grateful to my relatives, who supported us in every possible way during this critical time.

After my mother's passing, there was an overwhelming sense of emptiness at home. My father's behavior as an alcoholic kept worsening. Despite the emotional turmoil, I knew I had to keep moving forward. I began to take things one day at a time, slowly rebuilding my life with a focus on the future. I firmly believed that life would get better slowly over the next year, and gradually, we started healing from the accident.

My sister, Dhivya, decided to pursue her Bachelor's in Petroleum Engineering at Anna University. I hoped that her studies would give her a sense of purpose and help her cope with the loss. Her decision brought a glimmer of positivity into our lives, a small but significant step toward healing.

In September 2010, I received my offer letter from TriCent, with a joining date set for the 27th. The news was bittersweet; it signaled a new beginning, yet it came amidst the grief of losing my mother. I was determined to seize this opportunity, not just for myself, but for the sake of my family.

Physically, I was still recovering from the car accident, with my fractured right hand making everyday tasks a struggle. I had to rely on my left hand for everything, from eating to dressing, which took a toll on my patience and spirit. However, during this time, I found solace in Paulo Coelho's *The Alchemist*. The story of the shepherd boy who discovers that the journey itself is the true treasure resonated deeply with me. It reminded me that even in the darkest times, there's value in the journey, in the experiences that shape us.

As I prepared to embark on my professional journey with my first organization, I promised myself that I would work smarter, save diligently, and make the most of every opportunity that came my way. The challenges I faced during my college days, from navigating language barriers to overcoming the fear of public speaking, had equipped me with resilience. I knew the road ahead would be tough, but I was ready to face it with the strength I had gained from my experiences.

The journey from Madurai to Gurgaon was not just a physical move but a transition into a new phase of life. It was a step toward independence, a chance to create a future where I could stand on my own feet. And though the pain of loss lingered, I carried with me the lessons learned, the memories cherished, and the hope for a better tomorrow.

Nambirajan - Engineering in Coimbatore:

After completing my improvement, I attended the Engineering counselling where I chose Electronics and Instrumentation Engineering (EIE) in GCT (Government College of Technology) in Coimbatore. with that, the next four years of my life were sealed for Coimbatore. Now, let's be clear—my decision to pursue Electronics and Instrumentation Engineering had nothing to do with a passion for circuits or a lifelong dream of working in the electronics field. Nope. It was more like, 'Oh, there's one seat left? Well, that must be destiny calling!' It was an irrational decision, but it sure made for an interesting story.

Given that my elder brother had studied in PSG, Coimbatore, the choice of the city was a no-brainer. But the GCT Hostel wasn't exactly the lap of luxury. It was far from the cushy, comfortable experience you might expect from a hostel. The halls were fan-less, and the bathrooms... Well, let's just say they had a unique fragrance that no air freshener could fix. Yet, somehow, I survived the first two years with some table fans and as much as less use of the toilets as humanly possible. By the third and fourth years, I became a day scholar, and that chapter had its own share of adventures. But before we dive into that, let me tell you about the time I almost dropped out of

Engineering altogether.

After the first year euphoria of a new college and a new set of friends, in the second year a sense of resignation and depression began to set in. The truth is Engineering was not my cup of tea. I struggled in math, never really understanding most of the concepts. The other Electronics based subjects weren't also interesting to me. Studying about diodes, transistors and amplifiers never really excited me. I didn't bring the right context to my studies and my academics began to flag. What I only enjoyed was participating in quizzes outside of my college. Unlike Humanities, which often offer minors and majors, Engineering didn't have such distinctions. If it did, I'd say I majored in Quizzing and minored in barely scraping through exams.

College life was mostly a mix of mild depression sprinkled with occasional moments of joy. The peak of this emotional roller coaster was during my second year when I was denied a hall ticket for the first-semester exams due to low attendance. The principal summoned me, and instead of a pep talk, I got a full-blown shouting session. Without the hall ticket and not much motivation to study a subject I couldn't care less about, I decided to drop out. If Steve Jobs can drop out and be a tech leader and a billionaire, I can also be! The very next day, I was supposed to have a math exam, but instead, I took a bus to Chennai to meet my brother. Turns out, he wasn't there—he had gone to Tirunelveli. When my family realized the state I was in, they sent my uncle to pick me up and bring me back home to Tirunelveli.

I'll never forget my mother's tears when I walked back through the door. My father wasn't angry—just disappointed. They could see I was frustrated with Engineering and seriously considering dropping out. They asked what I wanted to do instead. My answer was 'Animation design'. I had developed a fascination with Pixar movies and was inspired by Apple and Steve Jobs. The last thing I wanted to do was go back to GCT. But somehow, they convinced me that finishing Engineering first and then pursuing animation would be a smart move. Reluctantly, I agreed and returned to GCT, though by that time, I had already missed three exams.

We stayed in a hotel near Coimbatore city center, where I crammed for the remaining exams, accompanied by my brother and father. Thanks to their support, I managed to scrape through the semester. After that, I moved back home to Tirunelveli for the semester holidays and officially became a day scholar from the next semester onwards. Now being more mature, I could see the value in completing stuff that you take on - sometimes irrespective of your like and dislike for it.

For the third year, we rented a room in Coimbatore, where my brother stayed with me. By the final year, I was living with friends, and that's how I managed to get through college. Despite missing many classes and not having much interest in Engineering, a few good things did happen during those Coimbatore days like the days of quizzing fun, the joy of discovering World Cinema movies in Konangal Film Society, learning about Isha yoga center, watching tons of TED videos and finally the memorable KBC (Kaun Banega Crorepati is the Indian version of Who Wants to be a Millionaire) shooting with Shah Rukh Khan (SRK). College time provided enough intellectual stimulation only that most of it happened outside the classroom. And the highlight of it - the KBC episode happened in Mumbai far away from Coimbatore.

I used to quiz very rarely in school, but quizzing became a regular part of my life starting in my second year of Engineering. I would often skip classes to participate in quizzes at various colleges in Coimbatore—winning some, losing others. Coimbatore's quizzing circuit has got many quizzes conducted by Prof. Rangarajan of PSG College of Arts and Science. I participated in some of these quizzes and managed to win some too. One of the highlights of my quizzing stint in Coimbatore was when our quiz team won the Coimbatore round of the IMS quiz and qualified for the national finals in Goa. This gave me my first flight experience—we flew from Coimbatore to Bengaluru. Later on, I would attend some quizzing clubs like QFI in Chennai and KQA in Bengaluru, and even worked as a Quiz Master for a brief period. Quizzing has remained a hobby of mine even now, though nowadays it mostly takes place on WhatsApp groups and online platforms.

The pinnacle of quizzing in my college days was my experience with one of the biggest TV shows in India during those times—KBC (Kaun Banega Crorepati). Modeled on *Who Wants to be a Millionaire*, it was initially hosted by Amitabh Bachchan (who still hosts the episodes). The third season of KBC, in 2007, was hosted by Shah Rukh Khan. The gameplay of KBC is very similar to that of *Millionaire*—if you answer a series of questions correctly, you eventually get to win 1 Crore rupees.

My obsession with *Kaun Banega Crorepati* started in 10th grade, and I kept applying each season. Finally, in my third year of Engineering, when Shah Rukh Khan was hosting, I got the call. I answered the phone-in question correctly and was selected for the studio round in Mumbai. I could bring one companion, so I took my elder brother. We were flown to Mumbai, where we stayed in a 5 star hotel. The episode was supposed to be shot on January 31st, but some celebrity appearances meant my episode was delayed to February 1st. When the day finally arrived, we were shuttled to a studio in a set inside a church. Shah Rukh Khan was charming as I expected him to be but the TV set seemed a bit small compared to the way its shown on TV. For people uninitiated about Bollywood, Shah Rukh Khan is one of the most popular actors in India who has acted in movies like Dilwale Dulhania Le Jayenge, My Name is Khan and Chennai Express. His movie 'Swades' where he acted as a NASA scientist who returns back to India is a movie that's close to all NRIs (Non Resident Indians) who live abroad but carry India in their hearts.

In the run up to the KBC appearance, I had refreshed my praathmic level Hindi. But it wasn't enough. Unfortunately, I flunked the Fastest Finger First round since the answer options were in Hindi. Considering all the efforts to reach the hot seat, it turned out to be a bit of a disappointing end. I made some errors in the play-along section and lost the 2 Lakh rupees prize money too. While going back we had some hiccup too in the flight back to Coimbatore. Overall it was a disappointing end to a dream. Despite the disappointment, it was an incredible experience—a childhood dream fulfilled. And yes, I still daydream about winning big on a game show one day.

SRK and me in the sets of KBC circa 2007

Here's my Fastest Finger First question: Arrange from top to bottom parts of the human body? The options that were all in Hindi were that of forehead, nose, palm and feet. It would have been a simple question for a native Hindi speaker. But for a person from Tamilnadu which has a long history of anti-Hindi agitations, it was a toughie and I got yorked in the Fastest Finger round. Later KBC would be run in Tamil too for a few seasons as 'Neengalum Vellalam Oru Kodi' (NVOK). But getting selected for the hot seat rounds in Tamil KBC didn't work either.

Now back to my college life. It was during my Coimbatore

college days that I joined the 'Konangal Film Society' and attended their movie screenings, where I discovered movie classics like *Rear Window, Dog Day Afternoon, The Seventh Seal.* I was captivated by the suspense created in *12 Angry Men*, all within the confines of a single room. Maybe it was just me escaping the boredom of college classes that made me want to watch a movie. Later, I began downloading films on my own, watching movies like *Groundhog Day* and *Back to the Future* from the IMDb Top 250 list. Now, with streaming services, there's something deeply fulfilling about diving into a well-crafted film that's both enlightening and joyful.

Thanks to my elder brother, I was also introduced to Isha yoga classes and the Isha Dhyanalinga during my GCT days. We used to visit the ashram at least once a month, back when it wasn't the nationwide phenomenon it is today. In fact, I later got married at the Isha Linga Bhairavi temple. Interestingly, while I maintain an interest in Isha, my brother has since become a staunch critic—oh, how the tables have turned.

No recollection of my college days would be complete without mentioning my misadventures in love—or rather, my attempt at it. Yes, I liked a girl in my class. But she was distant, and though we became somewhat friendly by the third year, it didn't last. After graduation, we went our separate ways—she joined a tech company, and I went to a multinational software services corporation, and we haven't spoken in decades. Looking back, I can see how immature and emotionally clueless I was. Let's just say, I lacked all the tact and nuance needed to navigate the complexities of love at that age. The less said about those crazy days, the better.

Apart from the *big memories*, there are countless 'little memories' from those days, each with its own unique flavor (quite literally in some cases):

- Devouring egg semiya at Akka Mess, sneaking in Mysore pa from Sri Krishna Sweets, thumping full meals at Ananda Bhavan in Gandhipuram, or demolishing litchis in RS Puram—*and* let's not forget the legendary half kaalaan at one of those glorious roadside eateries.
- Watching BSNL Sports Quiz like it was the World Cup final, all while clutching a melting ice cream bar—pure multitasking genius.
- Powering through initial training for BCS at a hotel in Coimbatore, passing through coding classes and exams.
- Discovering the city's unofficial 'start-up scene' of MLM schemes like QBiz, which sprouted in Coimbatore faster than a monsoon weed.

Each of these little moments is a quirky thread in the larger tapestry of my college days—days that came with their own set of challenges but were also sprinkled with fun, food, and a surprising amount of self-discovery.

3

Rookie Years - First Job's triumphs and tribulations

Sathya: *First job is when you start trying to figure your own home?*

Nambirajan: *More than creating your own home, you probably are staying with colleagues or friends. Your own home is still few years away.*

Sathya: *Yes, probably we all made mistakes in our first two years of working.*

Nambirajan: *I did too. That's why the phrase exists 'greenhorn' which refers to people who are just beginning their career and they are fresh and untested.*

Sathya: *Fresh to make mistakes. I have mentioned some of my mistakes in this chapter.*

Nambirajan: *What was your learning from that mistake?*

Sathya: *That I should know how to balance my emotions. I had some anger management issues in the initial stages of my career.*

Nambirajan: *Yes emotional regulation is often an overlooked aspect. I made some mistakes too in that area in my initial years.*

Sathya: *Maybe we can go right ahead and share our experience?*

Nambirajan: *Yes, let's end this standup scrum now and start our chapter.*

Sathya - My First Job Training Days at Gurgaon

I received my joining date for the first organization that specialized in creating software solutions for telecommunication brands—Tricent (name changed for privacy reasons). My first day of joining was September 27th, 2010, and the initial training was set in Gurgaon. With my dad recovering from his fracture due to the accident, he couldn't travel with me to Gurgaon, U.P. Nor could my relatives, who had a strong aversion to Hindi. Fortunately, my father managed to arrange a flight ticket for me, and I was set to fly from Coimbatore to Gurgaon. It felt like the safest option, given that the alternative was a two-day-long tedious train journey to Delhi.

I vividly remember my first flight alone from Coimbatore to Delhi. That was my golden ticket of opportunity. As I gazed at the fluffy clouds from the window, I promised myself that I would change my future and take many more flights for work and a better life. With that resolve, I bid farewell to Madurai and soared toward Delhi.

I landed at Delhi Airport at 7 p.m. My college batchmates, who had been through the training in the previous session, were there to help me with transportation, routes, and accommodation. The drive from the airport to Gurgaon was enjoyable; I marveled at the wide roads from the cab window. However, the next day, as I traveled to our Nalanda Training Centre in a rickshaw with my college friend Yatra, I was disappointed. Gurgaon, a dusty town on the border of Punjab and Delhi, did not meet my expectations. It was a hub for multinational companies because it was more affordable compared to Bangalore or Chennai, but it also had a reputation for various shades of crime. Gurgaon taught me survival and gave me a thick skin.

I spent three months living in Sector 12, in a ladies' paying guest accommodation with roommates Yatra and Kush (names changed). Having Yatra as a roommate was a relief, as she had previously traveled with me to BITS Pilani for a symposium. Occasionally, we would visit her home in Delhi for a taste of lemon rice, *rasam*, and other South Indian dishes.

During Nalanda training days in Tricent - a visit to Taj Mahal

In our class, there were only two Tamil-speaking students: Yatra and me. The rest were from other states of India and spoke fluent Hindi. Our classes were conducted in Hindi, as most students were Hindi speakers. Yatra was comfortable with this, but for me, the first month was challenging. I struggled to understand the concepts and often felt isolated. There were days when I cried out of frustration, but gradually, I adapted. After about a month and a half, I began to grasp the classes in Hindi and managed to negotiate with shopkeepers using my rudimentary Hindi. Students from Karnataka and Andhra could manage Hindi fairly well, but Tamil students found it particularly difficult. I felt this was a setback for Tamil Nadu.

Knowing Hindi would have given us an extra advantage for traveling within India without hurdles and fear. Thanks to Gurgaon, I learned this valuable lesson.

Alongside the language barrier, food was another struggle. I quickly grew tired of the daily chapati and brinjal sabji without rice. South Indians' everyday staple food is rice. Like most South Indians, we eagerly awaited the lemon rice packets sent by Yatra's mother every Monday. Those were stressful three months.

We had four core subjects: C, C++, Operating Systems, and Data Structures. Weekly exams were tricky and complex. I remember failing the first two exams (C and C++), but I aced Data Structures with a score of 99 out of 100. Data Structures had always been my strong suit. During this period, I discovered another batch of Tamil students, which felt like an oasis in the desert. Their presence brought joy and comfort. Some of us memorized Hindi phrases to communicate with shopkeepers, and we took breaks to visit landmarks like the Taj Mahal in Agra, Akshardham in Delhi, and Krishna's birthplace in Mathura.

Safety was a constant concern in Gurgaon. We frequently heard news about crimes against women. One Friday night, my Tamil friends faced a minor incident: while walking back to their hostel from my place, bottles were thrown from a house terrace, targeting them. Thankfully, they hurried past and reached their hostel safely. This incident shook us and reminded us to stay alert outside our hostel rooms. Gurgaon stripped away our small-town innocence and taught us the importance of vigilance.

As our training neared its end, we faced coding and debugging exams amidst the winter chill. This was my first encounter with North India's winter. In Tamil Nadu, we rarely wore sweaters or jackets unless we visited hill stations like Ooty or Kodaikanal. The cold in Gurgaon was unexpected, and I had to navigate it while preparing for my exams. The final coding exam required writing clear, well-commented code that could be easily understood by a schoolchild. It wasn't just about the output but about readability, efficiency, and clarity. This highlighted the gap between theoretical knowledge and practical application in the industry.

By then, I had received my stipend for two months. My first paycheck of 26,000 rupees was a significant milestone, and I used it to buy a laptop and cover my monthly expenses. The confidence from earning my own money was immense. From then on, I started to look after my expenses. I used the first laptop for coding practice and eventually passed my exams. I've seen students who sleep at training centers, coding day and night. Those were crazy days at Nalanda. I also passed the two subjects I had previously struggled with, all while avoiding the risk of being sent back for failing more than three times.

One of the final tasks involved building a project with a team of four, including two highly skilled coders, Ankit and Kishan. We ended up with 4,000 lines of code due to their high egos. We spent an entire night debugging 500 lines of errors before the presentation day. This experience taught me that writing clean and simple code requires clear communication and effective work division within a team, much like a coordinated stage performance.

Nalanda Training Centre taught me not only the nuances of software development in telecommunications but also invaluable life skills. Finally, we graduated to the next level, and I opted for deputation at the Bangalore office. I packed my bags lightly for the move in January 2011. My organization helped me book a flight from Gurgaon to Bangalore, marking the end of my Gurukul life in Gurgaon. (Gurukul is an Indian system where students live and study with their teachers, their guru).

And now to Nambi to share about his first work experiences and the memories from it.

Nambirajan - Getting placed in BCS and first work days:

In my final year of Engineering, I appeared for the 'campus interviews' — a set of assessments and interviews that happen over a few days when companies like BCS, CTS, and HCL visited GCT, Coimbatore to conduct aptitude tests and interviews to select candidates for their companies. It was 2007, and looking back, the recession that would hit the following year was far away. Software services companies like BCS (name changed, but it still rhymes) were recruiting in bulk. In my college, they would hire in a single year around 300-400 people out of a batch of 700+ students. Effectively, they were the largest recruiter in our college. Many students wanted to get into BCS, but the most academically oriented ones with high scores didn't — they preferred higher-paying companies like Microsoft or DE

Shaw, which would hire at most 2 or 3 people from the whole college. The pay packages at such companies were easily 10x what you would earn in a company like BCS.

I was an average student who had two backlogs/arrears that I still needed to clear. This made me only eligible to apply for BCS. I applied and got through. I was one of the 300+ people recruited in BCS that year. I wasn't overjoyed nor sullen about it. I was glad that despite all the struggles and incidents during my second-year exam dropout, I managed to scrape through and secure a job offer in my final year — a modest success. At the same time, I wasn't sure if I would fit in at BCS. I wasn't like most of my classmates. I read books they didn't, watched movies they didn't, and had ambitions they didn't. Perhaps it was just my youthful, naive thought that I was somehow special and different. This rebellious streak, which I would later understand through my Landmark Forum classes, came from my aversion to authority and the mainstream path.

Anyway, after completing my final year of Engineering with (not) flying colors and just about passing many subjects, I joined the Initial Learning Program (ILP) set by BCS in Coimbatore. These were two months of training sessions arranged by BCS in cities like Chennai, Bengaluru, and Coimbatore. I was eager to leave Coimbatore and get trained in Bengaluru or Chennai, but despite my negotiations, I was assigned to Coimbatore. So, I joined the ILP classes in the summer of 2008.

The two months of software coding and soft skills training passed, most of which I don't remember now. What I do remember is one of the soft-skill teachers telling us how to use perfume for our clothes and how to build our wardrobes — slowly over time, with good quality shirts and trousers. I met a few friends during this training, since we stayed in a hotel for those two months. I also got acquainted with Aaliyah (name changed), who also took the training in the same batch. We continued to stay in touch even after we joined our work projects in Chennai. But misunderstandings crept in, and we quietly drifted apart. She got married and moved elsewhere. Another 'Engirundhalum Vazhga' (Live Happily Ever After) story in my life.

After the two months of ILP, I joined the BCS office in Chennai and was assigned to 'Mainframe' — a legacy software program still running banking systems in the United States. I found it to be drab and relentless, but somehow completed the training and started in a production support project with Bank of America — one of the largest clients of BCS at that time. Production Support projects are those that occur once a software is already built, and this team takes care of 'repairing' any bugs that might arise. They were slightly boring compared to development projects, where you get the chance to build software from scratch.

At that time, BCS probably employed around two lakh people, with thousands working in Chennai. They had multiple offices across the city, and in 2008, they were about to complete building a massive office space in Siruseri that could easily seat 25,000 people across many buildings. When I joined BCS, it was still under construction, and by the time I left, some of the buildings in Siuseri HQ were complete. I initially joined BCS's Chennai One office in Thoraipakkam, then moved to the

Sholinganallur office, and finally worked in the Siruseri office.

Most of my time was spent on Bank of America (BoA) related projects. Looking back, I had many of the frailties of youth. I was careless about my work, showing up late on most days, not paying attention in meetings, and generally treating BCS as a temporary stop in what I assumed would later be a great career. This all came to a head in a now tragic yet funny incident during a quiz event — one that feels particularly appropriate for me to share. Let me recount this incident, hoping young people can learn from the mistakes I made years ago.

BCS used to host annual quiz programs called 'Couple of Questions' — a quiz event where you partner with someone of the opposite gender, either a colleague or a family member. I reached out to a few female colleagues I knew, but most of them weren't interested in quizzes. In a desperate attempt to find a partner before the quiz, I drafted an email expressing my desire to find a quiz partner for this event. Not knowing who to address it to since most female colleagues had turned me down, I picked a few email IDs of BCS colleagues from other emails and sent a cold email, which probably reached 60-70 people. Little did I know that this would set off a chain of events that would impact me.

On that fateful Friday afternoon, I received a call asking me to report to HR at around 3:30 pm. Since I was on the bench at the time, I was at home, and I thought this might be about a new project. So, I took the bus to the Chennai One office and went straight to the HR team. A manager, whose name I've since forgotten, asked me to wait in a conference room. After 10 minutes, he trudged in and immediately asked, "Did you write this email?" My heart sank. I had no idea what was coming.

I tried to explain myself — about the quiz and how I needed a female partner. He dismissed it as spam and told me I shouldn't have done it. And then came the bombshell: "You need to write a resignation letter, hand over your ID card, and leave the office now." I was completely shocked. I hadn't expected this. I argued that this was a BCS event, and my request was legitimate, but he kept repeating that it was spam and that I had to resign. I was at a loss for words and, in frustration, I stormed out of the meeting room.

I spoke to my manager, hoping for some support, but to my disappointment, he agreed with HR. He said, "People leave all the time; it's okay." I realized then that no one would stand by me. I felt dejected, and it was clear that my connection with BCS was broken. But I told them I would return on Monday to hand over my ID card. The weekend passed in a fog of depression. My hopes of having a successful first job were fading.

When Monday came, I returned to the HR office, ready to return my ID card. But another HR lady took me aside and suggested I write an apology letter, so I could continue with the company. I wasn't expecting this, and it gave me a glimmer of hope, but somehow, I knew this wasn't the way I wanted to leave. I wrote the apology letter, but deep down, I made the decision to leave BCS on my own terms within a year. My connection with the company had already broken, and it was only a matter of time before I would quit.

Looking back, of course, the HR manager and a few others at BCS overreacted to the email. But I also realized that I didn't have a strong context for dealing with incidents like this. In any career or team, you need a powerful context that guides your actions. Only then can you rise above temporary setbacks and failures. The right context gives meaning to your work and motivates you to perform well for both yourself and your team.

Even now, I don't feel strongly attached to any of the brands or offices I worked for (with the exception of Walmart, perhaps). After BCS, I worked on another project for a few months, but mentally, I had already switched off. I knew I would leave the company soon. I was planning to quit in around a year's time. This realization made me start looking at what I wanted to do next. Design had always interested me, although I had never been formally trained in it. I began exploring options to pursue a Master's at NID. My first attempt was for the Animation Design course. Though I cleared the initial exam, I failed the interview. The next year, I spent time exploring other design courses in India, feeling confused and vaguely roaming around the country. By now, my resume had a gap of about a year, but I wasn't too worried.

During this time, I stayed with my brother in Chennai, but things didn't work out, and I eventually moved out to stay with friends in Thiruvanmiyur. After some time spent being aimless, I found direction with some coaching from someone I met at the Landmark Forum. Thanks to that, I landed a job at a social media company in Mumbai. After working there for a few months, I transitioned to a quizzing company in Bengaluru.

Becoming a Quiz Master was a childhood ambition of mine, and the opportunity finally came when I was in Mumbai. I was meeting with a Quiz Master when he mentioned that Giri Balasubramaniam, a popular quiz master, was looking for a new Quiz Master for his company, GrayMaps. I applied and eventually got the job. Since quizzing had always been an area of interest, I packed my bags and moved to Bengaluru.

My experience at GrayMaps lasted about a year, filled with both highs and lows. On the positive side, I got the opportunity to travel to Muscat and host quizzes for the 'Times of Oman' quiz. I also contributed to the GK books that GrayMaps planned to release for school kids in India. But, during one heated moment, I lost my temper and shouted at a colleague. This incident escalated, and long story short, I was laid off. Although I would have liked to continue as a Quiz Master, I am grateful that the experience led me to again apply for NID in Bengaluru.

This time, I corrected the mistakes I made during my first application attempt — I applied for two courses instead of one, did all the preliminary work myself, and more. Studying at NID created the opportunity for a semester exchange in Zurich and later working as a Product Designer in Germany. This pivot from software executive to designer, via a brief career as a Quiz Master, is a story I'll elaborate on in a later chapter.

In 2008/2009, when I was first working in Chennai, I got involved with TEDxChennai. At that time, events like BarCamp — an unconference where the audience could volunteer to speak on a topic — were popular. I proposed that we could get a TEDx license for Chennai, which would allow us to host our own TED-style event. A group of us, led by Kiruba, who ran a Social Media and Digital Marketing firm, formed a team. The first TEDxChennai event at IIM Madras was a huge success. However, during the subsequent years' events, new organizers broke some TEDx rules, like allowing a sponsor to talk on stage and hosting a press conference. As a result, TEDxChennai was banned for two years. This was a big setback for those of us who had initiated the event. Although there have been efforts since then to revive TEDxChennai, it never really regained its momentum again. Retrospectively, Kiruba could have reined in the rule breakers who had joined the organising team. But in an effort to enlarge the impact, they made a few mistakes. Ironically this coincided with the 2 year ban of CSK, the IPL team from Chennai. Seemed like Chennai and 2 year bans go together.

One of the memorable experiences I had during my gap year between my first job at BCS and pursuing my post-graduation at NID was meeting Kiran Sethi, a designer and founder of the Riverside School in Ahmedabad. She gave a TED India talk about how children can create their own solutions for problems they care about. I was deeply inspired by her message and spent some time contributing to the Riverside campus initiatives. Riverside's 'Design for Change' program continues to inspire children to become designers and innovators.

Another extracurricular activity I took up during my working days in Chennai and Bengaluru was co-founding a book club called 'We Read Therefore We Are,' with my friend Shreedhar in Chennai. We even set up a Bengaluru chapter, where I met Sathya — more on that later. Through this book club, we organized a few meetups to discuss books. One of the highlights of our Chennai meetups was the chance encounter with AR Rahman, who happened to drop by during one of our gatherings.

Despite all the mistakes and small victories in my first jobs, my twenties were a crucial time for figuring out what I truly wanted to do with my life. Like they say 'Twenties are the best time to take risks in your life'. I did take them and I am happy for it now - one of them being quitting BCS and figuring my way into design. The 20s of my life were packed with experience of various colours and flavours, and through these experiences, I learned how to accomplish things later on. Needless to say - the early years, with their missteps, were an essential part of my growth.

4

Pivot Point - Embracing change in career

Sathya: *Pivot seems to have become a popular term*

Nambirajan: *Yes in startup parlance it means experimenting until you find out the way that works for you*

Sathya: *I pivoted from being a software developer to a Quality consultant*

Nambirajan: *That's not too much of a change*

Sathya: *What was your pivot?*

Nambirajan: *I went from being in software development field to being a designer*

Sathya: *Huh, that seems like a lot of change?*

Nambirajan: *There is similarity in change and there is change in* *similar profiles*

Sathya: *Before you get too philosophical, I am starting my pivot story*

Sathya: Bangalore Days and My Career Shift

After my training at Nalanda training center in Gurgaon, I opted for a deputation to Bangalore. In January 2011, I packed my bags and boarded a company-sponsored flight to Bangalore, a city that seemed like a breath of fresh air compared to the dusty streets of Gurgaon. Bangalore, with its vast, clean roads and lush greenery, felt like a new beginning. I often called it my New York, completely different from the city I had visited during a childhood trip years ago. The development was striking, with multinational company office buildings boasting glass facades stretching from Outer Ring Road to Whitefield. Yet, Bangalore still preserved its traditional neighborhoods like Jayanagar, BTM, and Basavanagudi. With these new surroundings, I embarked on my first project in Bangalore at a leading company, TriCent (name changed), in the telecommunications field at *Namma Bengaluru.*

Bangalore, the garden city of India, quickly fostered a sense of belonging. Most of my TriCent batchmates had also relocated to Bangalore, which made settling in easier. Hindi was no longer the only language I could easily navigate, since Kannada, Tamil, and English were widely spoken. This cosmopolitan nature made me feel more at home. My office, located near

Whitefield, was conveniently close to my Paying Guest accommodation, just four stops away. I lived near Kundalahalli Gate for about four to five years with friends like Chirax, my school friend Saranya, and a few other acquaintances. The traffic in Bangalore, particularly around Kundalahalli, became a significant frustration. On my visit in 2023, I was shocked to find that traveling from Electronic City to Sarjapur now took over two hours—one of the many downsides of Bangalore's rapid development.

I started as a developer on a telecom project involving networking protocols in routers. However, after six months, I realized the role wasn't as fulfilling as I had hoped. The lack of effective mentorship and the demanding office hours—often requiring me to stay late—started to take a toll on my health. Within eight months, I felt a growing sense of disillusionment and began exploring other roles within the company. I decided to try my hand at testing, where my job was to identify errors and bugs in the software code. I delved into automating manual tests, creating test plans, and using testing software. Unfortunately, the intense workload led to fatigue and a minor surgery due to the long hours.

In some projects at TriCent, I got a supportive team with a lot of empathy, learning together from mentors. In a few other projects, there was no professionalism—some members would come very late, very little information sharing happened, and there was no team camaraderie. These team members usually worked for their own self and career goals, often not helping any of the other team members.

But Chirax was different. Chirax was one of my project colleagues in my first project. She is from Assam, and I really loved her companionship. We later stayed at the same Paying Guest abode and shared a lot of travel memories, exchanging Bengali and *Tamil* cuisine, celebrating friends' birthdays together—it was a phase of fun. We had a bunch of batchmates like Jk, Chandru, Senthil, Uma, Akanksha, Mantri, and a few more friends. As we had little savings at that time, we rejoiced in smaller celebrations in a new city.

With only a year in the software field, I began considering other career options that aligned more with my interests and skills. Journalism or an MBA seemed like promising paths, as I enjoyed presenting and speaking. Initially, I pursued GMAT preparation and explored MBA programs. However, the exorbitant costs of Ivy League schools and the lack of specialization made me reconsider. An MBA seemed like a risky investment without a guaranteed return.

I took the next two years of my career as an exploration period. I was also thinking of options like journalism but remained skeptical. Despite my dissatisfaction with the software job, I gained valuable skills in team management, stakeholder management, conflict resolution, and assertiveness. I compared this phase to the internship concept in Germany, where high school students gain real-world experience in their chosen fields. This hands-on approach, which was missing in my education, was a revelation.

My career exploration led me to a pivotal moment when I encountered a member of the Software Quality Auditing and

Process Consultancy team. One day, while working at my first job, I came across a person who walked into my manager's cabin with a notebook and pen. My manager was patiently answering all his questions. I noticed this person regularly talking to my manager. Though he seemed to be a junior colleague compared to my manager, there was a lot of respect for him. When he visited, I sensed a bit of fear in the team managers. Out of curiosity, I began asking about his team and discovered that he was part of the software quality auditing and process consulting team, responsible for ensuring software development teams meet high standards of quality, efficiency, and compliance.

Intrigued by their work, I learned about a Master's in Quality Management program offered by BITS Pilani from my school friend Deva. Their course plan was more intuitive and interesting. The prerequisite for the course was that the candidate should be a working professional. Also, the thumb rule was that the candidate would not be able to pursue the course if they gave up their job during the two-year period. The course had 15 days of classroom sessions in a semester, followed by a closed-book exam, and then an open-book exam. The last semester was dedicated to thesis work. They had the concept of mentor selection from the organization, who needed to be an alumnus of this course. I loved the course design, and it was budget-friendly at 2.5 lakhs for the entire two years. This reasonable cost made it easy for me to pay for myself. I had saved some of my previous salary, which allowed me to complete the course without taking a loan or asking for help from my father.

Before starting this course, I approached my project manager to discuss a shift to the Quality Management team within TriCent.

Despite initial nervousness, I eventually gathered the courage to express my interest in joining the team and pursuing the WILP (Work Integrated Learning Program) from BITS Pilani. To my surprise, Saritha, the head of the Quality team, invited me for an interview. I accepted her offer. Within three months, I transitioned to the Quality Management team, where I found a better fit for my skills and interests. My new role was more aligned with my personality, and I enjoyed the work much more than my previous developer role.

Some acquaintances from the developer community advised me against this move into the field of auditing and process consultancy. Their reason was that I might not receive high pay packages and hikes like developers. Nevertheless, I felt it would suit my strengths and personality, as I was good at soft skills and could make a long-lasting impact in my career. I gave myself those two years to learn and experience the new field.

After two years, I still wasn't bored or exhausted as I had been as a developer. My master's program helped me apply concepts in real-time. I understood fundamentals like CMMI, ISO, metrics baselines, quality control tools, and more. This was also the time when the new phenomenon of Agile methodology was gaining traction in software circles, with the tagline 'What is your story?' I grew curious to learn about this concept, which deviated from traditional frameworks like CMMI.

My process consultancy team at TriCent provided excellent workshops on the Agile mindset across the organization. I was fortunate that our team head, Saritha, was also a psychologist specializing in transactional analysis (TA). She brought enormous focus on employee mindset while training the teams in Agile. I was introduced to psychology when I was 23 years old. At some point, I also got involved in imparting training on the Agile mindset, and I loved it. In short, Agile for me is where team psychology meets technology, and I felt this was where I could thrive.

During this time, I attended my 15-day classroom sessions at Peenya, Bangalore, for the Quality Master's program. Without taking leaves, my director made a flexible arrangement allowing me to log in for minimum hours per day during those sessions. I was running out of leaves at that point. I would wake up at 5 a.m., get ready, have breakfast, and leave around 6:30 a.m. for the classroom sessions. It was far from Kundalahalli, and I traveled in public buses for two hours. Classes ended at 3 p.m., after which I traveled to the Marathahalli office, reaching by 5 p.m. I refreshed at the office cafeteria and worked until 11 p.m. before the office cab dropped me at my PG around 11:30 p.m. Those were 18-hour workdays filled with travel, learning, and work.

During these hectic days, some helpful friends stood by me. I remember my friend Chirax saving food from the PG so I could have dinner after returning. Friends like her helped me manage those days meticulously. She was one friend who stood by me during my initial working days. I am grateful to have found friends like her early in my career.

One of the benefits of studying my master's program was the new friends I made. My batch was diverse, with people from different profiles and age groups. By the end of the first semester, I had a bunch of friends like Moushmie, Balaji, Hari, Sanjay, Bala sir, and Raja sir from fields like mechanical engineering, biotechnology, and software. Over those two years, the knowledge sharing from their fields enriched my understanding of quality management.

Defending the Masters thesis at BITS Pilani, Rajasthan

At this juncture, I made an impulsive decision to quit my job and change organizations. It was a hasty choice driven by anger. A heated argument with my Quality Head over an initiative I had undertaken out of interest escalated over the course of a week. My ego was strong at that time, and I didn't hesitate to engage in conflict with my manager. Although she eventually apologized, I didn't relent. Instead, I applied to other companies and received an offer within a week from a reputed multinational software services company. The salary increment wasn't significant for someone with 3.5 years of experience. Looking back, I realize I should have set my ego aside and approached the situation with greater composure. Walking away was easy, but standing firm and working through conflicts would have required patience and emotional regulation. I lacked in both of these at that time. This episode taught me the importance of maintaining emotional balance in both personal and professional settings.

Though I left my first organization, TriCent, in haste, it remains close to my heart. Mentors like Bindu and Benny guided me with fact-based decision making and supported me throughout my assignments. TriCent was also where I rediscovered hobbies that became integral to my life. I resumed Bharatnatyam classes in the evenings and started learning the musical instrument Veena at Purandhara Bhavan on weekends. I joined a book club, cultivating the habit of reading one book a month and making regular visits to bookshops. These small but significant habits enriched my routine. I even tried short treks to nearby mountains with friends like Chirax. Learning and practicing art made me a better person each day. Every Saturday, I attended Veena classes at Indira Nagar, Bangalore. The Veena, an ancient stringed instrument used in Carnatic music, was a rewarding yet brief pursuit for me. Even today, I continue Bharatnatyam classes in Berlin, thanks to the foundation laid during my time at TriCent.

My first day at the new organization, TechSyndra (name changed), lacked the vibrancy of TriCent. While 70% of TriCent's employees were young and brought energy to the workplace, TechSyndra had a more mature workforce, with many employees over 40. The atmosphere felt rigid and less cheerful—a stark contrast I shared with my manager, Kannan, as my first complaint.

During my time at TechSyndra, I had two mentors, Kannan and Saravanan, who continue to be my go-to advisors for professional guidance. A good mentor takes extra steps to support career growth, and both of them consistently challenged me with tough assignments while offering invaluable guidance. I also formed a lifelong friendship with Lalitha, my project lead. Though 10 years older than me, I initially thought we were the same age—a testament to her humility and approachability. From my mentors, I learned essential soft skills, such as handling people with respect and avoiding judgment. For instance, Kannan corrected me when I once giggled during a software quality audit—a moment that highlighted the importance of professional decorum.

Both mentors played a crucial role in my master's thesis, a six-month project requiring industry data and actionable recommendations. My thesis focused on attrition and how to reduce it in a scaled organization. Despite initial hesitance from HR to share sensitive data, my mentors proposed a sampling method that allowed us to gather departmental data and extrapolate it to a larger population. Together, we developed a process model, analyzed findings, and proposed recommendations. This experience deepened my appreciation for quality tools and data modeling, even though I wasn't naturally inclined toward quantitative analysis.

During this time, I also enrolled in a data science certification course at Jigsaw Academy. Although I didn't particularly enjoy working with data, I gained a basic understanding of its nuances and applications. My masters continued in parallel to my work and in the last semester I started my thesis work. My thesis defense took me to BITS Pilani, where my colleague Moushmie and I received a warm welcome, complete with air-conditioned guest accommodations to combat the Rajasthan heat. My thesis guide was impressed with our comprehensive work and even suggested I consider pursuing research at LEAD Graduate School in Germany.

Shortly after completing my master's degree, I received disappointing news: TechSyndra planned to dissolve the metrics team due to budget cuts. This challenging time highlighted the value of supportive mentors, as Kannan and Saravanan went above and beyond to help team members secure new opportunities. Their leadership was inspiring and reaffirmed the importance of having mentors who genuinely invest in their team's growth.

This period was also financially stressful. I was supporting my sister Dhivya's MBA program in Dehradun while managing my own living expenses and student loans. Specializing in Petroleum Management was a strategic choice for her, given the limited opportunities for women in fieldwork within the petroleum sector. Living paycheck to paycheck, I avoided asking my father for financial help, choosing instead to live frugally while ensuring my sister's education was funded.

After a year at TechSyndra, I secured a new position at a Governance, Risk, and Compliance (GRC) focused product company. This role came with a significant pay raise and the convenience of being located right opposite my PG accommodation. I also made a habit of saving, ensuring I had enough to cover at least three months of expenses. At this new company, I transitioned fully from software development to the Process and Audit team, marking a pivotal shift in my career.

Nambirajan: Pivoting to Design

I first heard about NID during my second year of engineering, thanks to Senthil, a career mentor who ran a coaching institute in Coimbatore. He introduced me to the National Institute of Design, one of India's premier institutions for learning design. However, I was already in my second year of engineering, which meant I would have to complete my degree before even considering a transition to design. Like millions of Indian students, I was on the well-trodden path of 'Do engineering first, then figure out what you really want to do.'

NID, hailed as the premier institute for design in India, was highly sought after by those genuinely passionate about design. Senthil believed my maverick ideas and unconventional approach would make me a great fit for the field. At the time, I was still recovering from the fallout of my failed attempt to drop out of engineering, so the idea of becoming a designer seemed both distant and tantalizing—a dream and perhaps a much-needed distraction.

After graduating from engineering, I was as uncertain as ever about my future. So, I decided to "go with the flow" and joined BCS (name changed) in Chennai. It was one of the topmost IT services company in India. While immersed in the IT world, I continued to nurture my dream of studying design. Looking back, I spent too much time searching for purpose instead of acting on it—time that could have been better spent figuring out NID's admissions process sooner. It taught me a critical lesson: going with the flow will only take you where the flow leads. To carve your own path, you often need to swim upstream, pause to reflect, and take intentional actions.

Two years into my job in Chennai, I finally applied for the Master's program at NID, focusing on animation design (I later realized I could have applied to two courses simultaneously). Clearing the DAT exam wasn't too difficult, and I was thrilled to be shortlisted for the interview at NID's Paldi campus. However, the interview itself posed a significant challenge. I had no idea what to expect or on what criteria the candidates were selected. Determined to give it my best shot, I booked a flight to Ahmedabad and arrived at the iconic NID campus.

In preparation, I enrolled in a small coaching center. Unfortunately, I realized their expertise was tailored for undergrad applicants, not post-grad aspirants. During this time, I came across the term "portfolio" and its significance in the design world. At NID, I saw candidates carrying thick binders of sketches, drawings, and finished projects—some had mock storyboards, printed ads, or even puppet storytelling portfolios. One candidate brought a guitar and performed during the interview. In contrast, I had no portfolio to speak of. Years of chasing academic marks had left me with little time to nurture or document my creative skills.

With only a few days left before the interview, I scrambled to create a portfolio, sketching comics about my time in Ahmedabad. I knew it was inadequate, but it was the best I could manage in such a short time. On the interview day, I presented my comics and drew a quick sketch of Shekhar Mukherjee, one of the panelists. When asked why I had joined a coaching institute and not believed in myself, I mumbled some answers. The truth was I lacked confidence in my creative abilities. The interview concluded, and when the results came out a month later, I wasn't selected. Needless to say, I was disappointed.

Returning to Chennai, I continued working at BCS for a few more months. As planned, I submitted my resignation in January 2010. What followed was a period of idleness. The steady paycheck stopped, and I began running out of savings. My search for a suitable design course remained as unstructured as ever, with Srishti and a few other institutes on my radar. Meanwhile, my brother, recently back from South Africa, was moving forward in his life—joining IBM, getting married, and settling in Madipakkam. In contrast, my own life felt stagnant. Eventually, I had to leave my brother's place and crash with a friend in Thiruvanmiyur.

Around this time, I had a revelation, thanks to some coaching from my mentors at Landmark: maybe it was time to stop chasing the ideal design course and take a job instead of wasting more time. So, I accepted a role as a social media executive at a firm in Mumbai. The social media boom was at its peak in 2010, with brands eager to establish their online presence and engage with customers. It was a burgeoning field, and I thought it might serve as a stepping stone.

During this stint, I reconnected with a friend from my quizzing days who told me about a job opening as a quizmaster at GrayMaps, a company run by the renowned quizmaster Giri Balasubramaniam. Quizzing had always been a passion of mine, so I applied and got the job. This opportunity led me to Bengaluru, where I spent an exciting year hosting quizzes and thoroughly enjoying the experience.

However, after a year at GrayMaps, things took an unexpected turn. I was laid off just as I was gearing up to host a quiz series in Tamil Nadu for *Puthiya Thalaimurai.* The setback hit hard, but it reignited my determination to pursue my dream of studying design. I revisited NID's application process, this time with better preparation. I applied for two courses at NID Bengaluru: 'Design for Digital Experience' (later rebranded as Interaction Design) and 'Information Design.' Learning from my earlier mistakes, I invested time in creating a robust portfolio that showcased my creativity and skills. My preparation paid off, and I cleared the exams and interviews.

Finally, in June 2013, five years after completing my engineering degree, I joined NID Bengaluru. It was a long-awaited milestone, marking the beginning of a new chapter in my life. This journey from wanting to join a design course during my

Engineering course to actually joining one took me almost 8 years - a journey filled with duty, detours, distractions and a lot more.

Reflecting on my journey, there are a few things I wish I had done differently:

- **Circa 1996:** Start aiming for NID right after school by cultivating my artistic and creative skills alongside academics.
- **Circa 2006:** Visit NID Ahmedabad while at GCT to understand their selection process and plan my preparation accordingly.
- **Circa 2010:** Follow up on a senior's advice to explore NID Bengaluru earlier and gain firsthand insights about the campus.

Had I taken these steps, I could have fast-tracked my career by several years. While my detours brought valuable life experiences, I often wonder how different things might have been if I had pursued design with a clear and focused vision from the start. All the stumbles and detours could have been avoided.

Onam celebration at NID, Bengaluru

Studying at NID provided its own strengths—one of which was the opportunity to meet and study with students from different regions of India. During my engineering days, most of my classmates were from Tamil Nadu. At NID, students came from almost every state in India. NID's mode of exams was also different. No longer did we have to write traditional exams like in engineering. Instead, they were replaced by the 'jury' system—a day when all students presented their work to a panel comprising professors and an external jury member. Additionally, NID, influenced by the Bauhaus movement relied heavily on workshop-based learning. Bauhaus is a pioneering Design movement created in the Weimar republic, Germany and is known for its simplicity and the philosophy 'form follows function'. In my first year in NID, many guest lectures and sessions were held where we learned the fundamentals of design and the design process. These workshops culminated in the creation of artifacts based on what we had learned.

NID provided a basic understanding of design principles and processes, but I learned just as much—if not more—from my peers as from the classroom sessions. A jury feedback session led me to explore design literature, which is how I discovered *Don't Make Me Think* by Steve Krug—a seminal work in usability testing for interaction design. I got introduced to indie games like *Fez* and *Super Hexagon* through a batchmate and later attended an indie game conference in Berlin. The NID library was also well-stocked and intellectually stimulating.

Life at NID wasn't without its pitfalls. I made my fair share of mistakes and learned from them. There were unnecessary distractions like 'interaction' (a euphemism for ragging) that only fostered resentment toward seniors. A student-led jury created emotional turmoil for me, and the ILP program from Landmark, which I had hoped to complete, ended in failure as well.

Amid the distractions and failures, there were joyful moments too. I learned the fundamentals of the design process, from ideation to testing. I discovered the joys of video-making—from conceptualization to editing, often spending hours perfecting my projects. I even created *NIDB Diary*—a video series documenting happenings at NID Bengaluru. I also led a few *Gyaan Adda* sessions, which introduced people from diverse fields to share their ideas with students on campus.

One of the highlights of my NID journey was my semester exchange in Zurich. This experience played a significant role in shaping my family's eventual move to Germany. Let me share some of that experience.

It was the 2014–15 academic year when a few batchmates traveled to Canada for an exchange semester. I applied but wasn't selected. Later in 2014, I applied for a semester exchange in Zurich and was fortunate to be accepted. Some friends warned me about Zurich's high cost of living, but I decided to go for it anyway. I believed exposure to a new environment and culture would enrich my design learning.

On January 26, 2015, I packed my bags and boarded a flight to Zurich, with layovers in Doha. Bengaluru was chilly in January, but as the plane descended into Zurich, I was greeted by a snow-blanketed landscape. I had never seen anything like it before. A fellow design student from Srishti also arrived on the same exchange program and was greeted by her family friends. I, on the other hand, had no relatives or friends in Switzerland. Luckily, a ZHDK student I had contacted earlier agreed to host me for a few weeks. She picked me up after a short delay, and we traveled by train and bus to her home in Affoltern, a Zurich suburb.

Having never traveled outside the Indian subcontinent (except for a rare visit to Muscat), everything felt new to me—the clean railway stations, punctual trains, and snowy winter streets. And then there were the expenses! At the time, the Swiss Franc traded at around 86–87 INR. Like many Indians abroad for the first time, I quickly developed a habit of mentally converting prices. A 7 CHF train ticket? That's 602 rupees for a train ticket. A sandwich for 9 CHF? That's a ₹774 sandwich. I quickly realized my previous spendthrift habits wouldn't work here.

For the first time, I started budgeting—tracking my income and expenses in a diary. This was a significant change from my college days when I spent freely without much thought. While working in Chennai and Bengaluru had taught me some financial discipline, Zurich forced me to truly appreciate the value of money.

My stay at my host's home began in February. Initially, I was supposed to stay for 2–3 weeks before finding alternate accommodation. However, staying elsewhere would have meant a significant expense, with monthly rent for a shared apartment (WG) costing 400–500 CHF. On top of that, transportation was another unavoidable cost. Living on the outskirts of Zurich meant I needed a Zone A/B/C ticket for trains, buses, and trams, which cost around 180 CHF per month.

I tried reaching out to Indian expatriates and other students for help related to accomodation, but nothing panned out. Finally, I managed to convince my host to let me stay until the end of the semester. Thankfully, she agreed.

My exchange semester batch in ZHDK, Zurich

The next major problem was loneliness. Though I had a set of fellow students in my game design discipline in my college, I found it difficult to make friends. Maybe it was the language barrier, I had very limited vocabulary in Swiss German. Or maybe it was the fact that they knew exchange students wouldn't stay beyond a few months and they didn't want to invest their time. Whatever may be the reason, those few months in Zurich were some of the loneliest days I have spent. Through the winter depression and the loneliness, I soldiered on to complete my semester.

Amidst the loneliness, winter depression and high costs of living, Zurich was a learning experience. One of my learnings was the presence of a high number of Sri Lankan Tamil people who had moved from their homeland to flee the war between LTTE and the Sinhalese army. This had happened over decades in the 80s and 90s leading to a creation of a new immigrant community in Zurich and many cities of Switzerland. Though I had heard about them previously, this was my first time seeing and interacting with them in flesh and blood. I learnt about how many of them toil in the hospitality industry as dishwashers without having an opportunity to rise through the ranks. Though they had left their homeland, some of them harbored a strong affinity to Tamil culture and continued many of their cultural aspects in a foreign land.

Zurich was the place where I met Viswanathan Anand. In the very first week of my stay in Zurich, I searched in twitter for '#Zurich' and found that there is a chess tournament happening in a hotel in downtown Zurich, not far from my place. I went there and during one of the game breaks I met Vishy, the Sun in the universe of Indian chess. He was casual and spoke to many Indians and even took selfies with them.

I also discovered a bit of Bollywood accidentally while on a students cultural visit to a place called Appenzeller. While visiting one of the cheese factories, a fellow Indian student saw a cow bell hanging on one of the ceilings and mentioned DDLJ. Being a Tamil guy I had never seen DDLJ (Dilwale Dulhania Le Jayenge) and went back to my place, watched the movie and realized the movie is set in Europe and more specifically in Switzerland. I googled for places that were shown in the movie which included many spots in Zurich and Switzerland. DDLJ was one of the movies in the wave of 90s movies whose songs were shot in Switzerland. The scene was so big that there is a statue of Yash Chopra, one of the acclaimed Bollywood directors in Interlaken, a touristy picturesque place in the west of Switzerland.

There were many things about Zurich which were new and unique for me. For example their political system where they rotate the role of the Prime Minister among 12 council members. Their focus on cleanliness and punctuality ensured almost all the train stations were clean and the bus, trains arrived on time. Switzerland also had four official languages - Swiss German, French, Italian and Romansh (which is spoken by less than 1% of the population). Personally speaking, I found the Swiss people to be a little cold and reserved - the saying 'too quiet, too rich' about Zurich natives wasn't inaccurate.

One of the good things which happened during my semester exchange was the opportunities to travel. I traveled to Barcelona and Paris for a visit to the city and I also visited Berlin to attend a game design conference. It was an Indie game conference called 'Amaze' and I got a kind host who hosted me for a few days for the conference. I took a Flixbus which was an 8-hour ride from Zurich to Berlin. The conference was a learning experience where I got to meet the doyens of the Indian game world like the creator of Super Hexagon, a game I played in NID. I also met a few NID Paldi students who were doing their semester exchange in German universities. I had no idea that I would visit Berlin later in my life. But while leaving Zurich, I realized many of my struggles had money at its core and decided to return to Europe as a working designer. I put this seed in the back of my head and continued with my life. Seven years later I would get that opportunity to work as a product designer in

Europe.

Receiving my Post Graduate degree in design from author Ramachandra Guha circa 2017

By June 2015, my semester exchange was done and I packed my bags, waved my final goodbyes, and took the flight back to Bengaluru. Fresh off my trip, I joined for internship at SAP Labs, Bengaluru. Meanwhile, I completed my final thesis as well. I attended the campus placements in NID, Paldi and got selected to work in two companies. I chose to work in HeyTm and thus began my chapter of work in India as a product designer.

5

Joyful recollections of Trauma

Sathya: *That's a unique chapter title. How did you got this title?*

Nambirajan: *It's not my idea. I recently heard about this book 'Joyful recollections of Trauma' by an American comedian, actor, film maker, and podcaster Paul Scheer. I liked the title - how you can approach a serious subject like trauma in a funny, light hearted way. So here we are joyfully recollecting our traumas.*

Sathya: *That's nice. I have had quite a few small and big traumas in my life*

Nambirajan: *If you had to choose one, which incident would you pick?*

Sathya: *More than an incident, I would like to pick a theme which was there almost throughout my life from my childhood days. I have shared about it in detail in this chapter. What is the trauma that you want to share?*

Nambirajan: *I have a few stories which I can share. Some about natural disasters, another about man made traumas.*

Sathya: *that seems interesting*

Nambirajan: *yes Trauma when viewed from the future reflectively helps you identify what your values are especially if you had healed from it. But when they are happening...*

Sathya: *They are well... traumatic. Let me start my trauma story*

Sathya: Alcoholic Father, Therapy, and Rehabilitation

My father, Balakrishnan, is a self-made man who seems to have lived a life without fear. A quick look back at his life reveals a man of resilience and determination. During his B.Sc. in Mathematics, he defied his family to marry my mother, Shanthi. Starting with just 1,000 Rupees, he ventured into business to support our family. Initially, he sold clothes from a bicycle, despite having a degree in Mathematics. His passion for business drove him forward, and as his business began to grow, so did his exposure to bad influences. Alcohol became a part of his life, a habit he struggled to control. At one point, he got addicted to alcohol. Though he tried various methods to get rid of the addiction, it continued. Despite periods of sobriety, including a two-year stint in yoga, he would invariably relapse.

Me (on the right) with my father and sister

While growing up with such an alcoholic father, the turbulence at home was constant. Frequent fights and physical abuse became a norm. My mother, despite her efforts, was unable to shield my sister *Dhivya* and me from the chaos. The tension turned many nights of peaceful sleep into a nightmare. I often bore visible bruises, which I would hide from friends and teachers by claiming they were accidental injuries. This environment fueled my determination to excel academically as a means to escape *Madurai.* After my mother's death in the accident, my father's guilt drove him further into alcoholism.

As I began earning from my first job, I supported *Dhivya's* education, enabling her to pursue a Master's in Petroleum Management at Dehradun. Being financially independent allowed me to assist her with an educational loan and personally enroll her in her program. My father supported us to the extent he could, though his struggles with alcohol were ongoing. Despite his flaws, he was a man of paradoxes. He prioritized our education, supported other financially struggling children, and occasionally treated us to vacations in southern India like Bangalore, Mysore, *Ooty*. When he was sober, he would take us to nice fine-dining experiences in *Madurai*. Also, he bought many books for us from the book exhibitions. I read some of the books by *Iraianbu*, ex-IAS officer in India who writes motivational books for students. He made sure to visit book exhibitions whenever they were displayed in *Madurai*. He himself read the book *Rapidex English Speaking Course*, a book that helps to improve spoken English. I believe my intention to do charity sometimes would have come from him. No person is totally good or totally evil. We see shades of all in a person. For me, that person was my father who had his own good and bad qualities.

In 2015, feelings of emptiness and anxiety about my future led me to explore therapy, thanks to a recommendation from my former team director, *Saritha*. I began attending Transactional Analysis (TA) sessions with therapist *Lakshmi* in Bangalore. After four or five sessions, I was profoundly grateful for the experience. TA, developed by Eric Berne, analyzes social interactions to understand the communicator's ego state and address emotional issues. The therapy provided insights into unresolved grief over my mother's death, the shame linked to my father's alcoholism, and my fear of marriage stemming from witnessing my parents' troubled relationship.

Lakshmi guided me in addressing these issues. She advised me to accept my father's alcoholism as a disease beyond my control and to separate my own feelings from his condition. I learned that unresolved emotions can cause imbalances in our mental and physical health. By writing about my grief and embracing my emotions, I began to feel more balanced and authentic in social settings. Therapy also encouraged me to consider building a family, despite my earlier fears and hesitations about relationships. At 27, I took control of my own future, exploring options through matrimonial portals while remaining committed to finding a suitable partner.

During my therapy, I met Nambi at the Landmark Forum. Known from the book club days, his honesty and simplicity appealed to me. We dated for six months, navigating our own challenges together.

By the fourth therapy session, I recognized my father's condition as a chronic issue. We tried to bring him to live with me in Bangalore, but the attempt was unsuccessful. My sister and I came to accept him as he was. A relative enrolled him in a rehabilitation center in *Madurai*, where he began to receive the help he needed. Rehabilitation centers play a crucial role in assisting alcoholics and drug addicts to regain normalcy. From 2014 to 2024, he cycled through rehab centers, undergoing various treatments and counseling. In 2023, he managed to live independently in *Madurai* for a full year without alcohol. He recently celebrated his 60th birthday. But soon after that, he again relapsed into a fit of drinking.

Drinking not only spoiled my dad's health, it also led him to lose control and get into fights with people on the street. It also created issues with his relatives. His social life in *Madurai* got impacted because of his alcoholism. Many of my relatives are not on speaking terms with him. The cycle of being sober, not drinking alcohol for some time, then relapsing and spoiling his physical and social health seems never-ending. It's also a very prevalent issue in *Tamil Nadu* because of TASMAC shops, which are run by the government.

In such an environment, institutions and organizations that provide support for alcoholic people to recover are very few. One of them is AA - Alcoholics Anonymous - a chapter of which exists in *Madurai*. Alcoholics Anonymous (AA) provided significant support for him since circa 2022. It helped him refrain from drinking through community sharing sessions. AA is a fellowship that assists individuals in overcoming alcohol dependence through free meetings focused on sobriety. However, despite his progress, he relapsed and returned to rehab for another six months in 2024.

This journey deepened my interest in psychology. I began reading books like 'I'm OK, You're OK', 'The Body Keeps the Score' and recently attended a TA01 session. TA explores the impact of childhood experiences on adult behavior. I learned that many psychological issues stem from unmet emotional needs in childhood. My father's lack of parental care and unclear boundaries during his upbringing likely contributed to his alcoholism. Nonetheless, we hold on to hope, recognizing that it took a decade for him to accept his addiction as a disease and begin participating in AA sessions. We continue to support him and remain hopeful for his full recovery.

As a society, the Government and other non-government organizations and institutions have to think about creating and setting up as many rehabilitation centers at subsidized prices to take care of the hordes of people suffering from addiction. We have a lot of TASMAC shops selling alcohol, but I have seen only two or three rehabilitation centers in *Madurai*. Personally, in my family, we would have spent 15 lakhs in this period of 12 years. I can imagine the plight of people who don't make enough money even for their survival but also have to take care of their alcoholism issue. The awareness of rehabilitation centers and 'Alcoholics Anonymous' community is diminishing. A healthy society can be created only if we take the necessary steps to correct societal issues and prevent them with therapy centers. As my dad has a small business and a home, his business assistants keep track of his health by visiting him once in a while. This might not be an option for many others who work in manual labor for whom every day not spent working is a day without any income. In such a scenario, the financial health of such families is also impacted. Hence, the government has to make more measures to support them in their journeys to get cured of this addiction.

Alcoholism is not just my personal trauma but a trauma that impacts millions of people in India and around the world. My hope and prayer is that individuals who suffer from alcoholic addiction find the necessary support and remedy that will enable them to come out of their addiction and lead healthy lives.

Nambirajan: Improvement, Flood and the tenant trauma

Trauma 1: The year long trauma - My year of improving!

I had shared about how I bungled my 12th exams by scoring only 93 percent and missing the qualification for prestigious medical college. After this happened, my father started to slowly push me to the option of 'improvement'—a fancy term for redoing your 12th grade and reappearing for both theory and entrance exams. Repeating a year of academics might seem simple, but it came with its own challenges and struggles, both physical and mental. Let me share more about that.

It was 2003, and the system then was a two-part ordeal: first, we took all our theory exams, then we gave our multiple-choice type questions in entrance exams. The two scores from theory and entrance were combined to get a cutoff out of 300. My goal was clear: I needed to score 296 or above out of 300. But here's the thing—when you're already in the 90th percentile, every single mark becomes a Herculean task. Moving from 60 to 80 is a breeze compared to clawing your way from 94 to 96, and inching up from 96 to 99 is like climbing Everest's last leg.

There were a few 'centers' in Tamil Nadu where such improvement students flocked. One of the most popular was SRV near Rasipuram in the Namakkal district of Tamil Nadu. In these improvement centers, private coaching and tests would happen through the next one year, and the students would again appear for exams. Exams were themselves pressure, and since we were doing it all over again, the pressure was even higher. A constant reminder at these 'concentration camps' for students was hauntingly simple: "Miss one five-mark question, and your chance is gone. An entire year wasted."

Life at SRV was quite drab. It was a place with a handful of big-name teachers like *Kanakavel* and *Ramaswamy. Kanakavel* was the chemistry teacher, running classes from his home, which doubled as a hostel. Picture this: about 15 kids crammed on each floor, 30 to 40 kids in total, all packed into this house for a year. And that was just one of the many mini-hostels. Across the town of *Rasipuram*, there were easily 400 to 500 kids all doing the same thing—cramming, stressing, and trying to claw their way to that elusive cutoff and get that prestigious medical seat. Rasipuram was a small town that had gained notoriety as an 'improvement center.' I heard that recently, after the Tamil Nadu government changed the rules and did away with the improvement system, these places probably stopped being improvement concentration camps. But when I was there, it was a full-blown industry.

It was like a mini South Indian version of Kota, the Rajasthani city known for IIT aspirants preparing for exams for many years. Luckily, improvement was time-boxed—you have a year and that's it. Through the year, it was either exams and classes. Exams are more than classes because you have already completed a year of studying in classes. So almost every other month, you would have exams which reached a crescendo just before the final board exams happened. I 'improved' along with

Nirmal and Praveen Daniel who were from my same school. We were in the same hostel and gave exams together. I used to score a little better than him in most exams, but in the end, he scored higher in board exams and now works as a doctor in Tirunelveli. I am happy for him—at least one of us got to complete our goals after sacrificing a year. Praveen Daniel was like me, didn't cross the qualifying bar and didn't become a doctor.

Here's what a typical day in SRV, Rasipuram looked like - a riveting saga of academic survival and caffeine-fueled desperation:

1. Wake up around 7 am, looking like a zombie that's been hit by a textbook truck, and zombie-walk to the *Ramaswamy* center for tea/snacks. That's where my friend *Praveen* studied - misery loves company, after all.
2. Return and study, attempting to cram formulas, facts, and concepts into my brain that was already screaming, "No more! I surrender!" Brain cells were dying faster than mosquitoes in a bug zapper.
3. At 9 am, shuffle off for breakfast, more out of a biological imperative than actual hunger. Like any self-respecting hostel, the food was firmly in the 'could sustain life, but might make you question that life' category. Chef Venkatesh Bhat would have had a breakdown.
4. Back to the books for a few more hours, lost in a monotony so thick you could cut it with a scalpel - how ironic for aspiring doctors.
5. Lunch at 1 pm - a brief intermission in the endless study marathon. Join a hundred other students in a feeding

frenzy that looked more like a scene from a nature documentary than a civilized meal.

6. More studying - because apparently, sleep and sanity are overrated luxuries for medical aspirants.
7. Evening classes from 5 pm to 7 pm, where keeping my eyes open was an Olympic-level sport. Blinking was a luxury, staying awake was the gold medal.
8. Dinner, followed by - you guessed it - more studying. Because why have a social life when you can have equations and anatomical diagrams as your best friends?
9. Finally, collapse into bed around 11 or 12, hoping to recharge for another day of this academic boot camp. My pillow became my most intimate relationship.
10. Dream about getting enough marks to get into a medical college and become a doctor - finally. Because nothing says "sweet dreams" like the hope of one day escaping this study prison.

Motto of SRV: Eat. Study. Survive. Repeat.

And that was my life for an entire year. The endless cycle of cramming and studying, with no attention whatsoever given to any hobby or art or anything else—how could there be, with hundreds of kids all fighting for the same thing? Even health took a backseat to studies. I was left to my own devices, and in this dull, drab world, I began to lose weight. My dad visited once, and I remember the look on his face when he saw me—lean and tired. He cried, seeing how much weight I had lost. But by then, it was too late to turn back. It was around December, and in a few months' time, the board exams and our final obstacle would have to be crossed. The choice my father had made for me was in reality, and I was too deep in to consider any other alternative.

I don't remember much else from that year—probably a good thing. Occasionally, we would escape the cramped study rooms and find a spot outside a nearby marriage hall to study, just for a change of scenery. Some kids would go to a nearby temple and study there, probably seeking divine spiritual intervention along with their studying. As the final months approached, my health took a nosedive from all the stress. I developed an anal fissure just before the exams—a painful condition that made it nearly impossible to focus during the tests. I still remember sitting for one of my language exams, wincing in pain with every word I wrote. But somehow, I got through it and completed all the exams and entrance tests. The stress had taken a toll on my health. Somehow, I survived both the theory exams and the entrance exams.

A few months later, the results came in. Initially, I scored 294/300 from both the theory and entrance combined. Then, as luck would have it, someone sued in court over a disputed question, and the court revised the answer key. My entrance marks dropped. This happened not once, but twice more. Finally, my score settled at 293/300. I had to score at least 296 and I scored only 293. The three-mark gap meant I had not qualified for studying to be a doctor. And with that, my dream of studying at Tirunelveli Medical College came to an end.

With no other choice, I turned to engineering. Since I had studied science and given all exams, my Engineering cutoff improved. My elder brother, who had studied at PSG College in

Coimbatore, suggested I aim for either GCT or CIT in Coimbatore. And I chose the former.

So there you have it—my year of 'improvement,' a year filled with stress, struggle, and ultimately, a disappointing result and finally a change in course. It's funny to think that all of this was because of an obsession with becoming a doctor. But that's how life is sometimes—you think you're headed in one direction, and then life hands you a detour.

Trauma 2: The recurrent trauma of floods

One of the most memorable days in my childhood life was something which happened in 1992 when I was around six years old. I don't know the exact dates when it happened, but that was the first time I experienced floods. Our home is situated around 2 kms from the banks of *Thamirabarani* river. Our home was situated in such a way that if you drew an imaginary line from our main door, it would reach the bank with no man-made structure in between. Though there is a stretch of '*mullkaadu*' (a patch of land with thorny bushes and trees in between the river and our home), it was very much possible that the river waters, if it flooded, would reach our home.

On that fateful day in 1992, the clouds were dark, and we could see the river water slowly gaining ground and reaching towards our home. There were talks of Manimuthaaru dam being opened to make sure the water doesn't damage the dams. My father was a bit complacent and was like 'these waters will never reach our home'. Around 2 or 3 pm, the water was about 700/800m away from our home. My father was still in his 'this will never reach our home' complacency. By evening, the water was close to our compound walls, and only then did panic kick in. A little too late, a little too much. We scampered to put some things above the loft so they would be safe. The TV was moved to the loft, and so were some clothes. Some heavier things like the fridge and bed were just left as is. My parents asked me to go with a person who lifted me and my brother on his shoulders and took us to a home nearby which was on higher ground. I still remember being lifted by that person (blessed be his soul) and being carried on his shoulders while water kept lashing till about his knees. The water eventually went as high as the chest level of an average person inside our home. And it took time to recede as well.

The next two weeks were spent in our relative's home. There was no school for those days, and my brother and I kept playing among ourselves. My parents probably stayed in another home. Two weeks passed like this, and finally, my parents came and took us back to our home. By now, the waters had totally receded, but there were a lot of things which got damaged. The walls still had a line marking the level to which the water had entered our home. Slowly but surely, we resumed our day-to-day life activities, and things came back to normalcy. Since I was a kid, I wasn't fully aware of the impact of these floods.

Fast forward to December 2023. We as a family made a trip to India from Germany. The idea was to stay in my hometown *Tirunelveli* for about 10 days and then in *Madurai*, Bengaluru before moving back to Germany.

So we landed in Bengaluru. And since Lufthansa messed up our baggage delivery, we had to wait one more day and then get our bags. We got the bags and then took a bus ride and moved to *Tirunelveli* around December 14. We met some of our relatives and were relaxing in our home when the Saturday of December 18 came.

It was raining the whole day, and we thought at some point it would stop. So we stayed indoors the whole day. It was just another lazy Saturday when we watched some movies on TV (another mistake not catching up on local news) and were about to sleep. Around 10 pm at night, we saw people coming up near our home and looking in the direction of the river. We opened our doors and took a look. That's when the coin dropped. The rains throughout the day had caused the river level to rise, and through one corner in our compound wall, the water was already coming into our compound. We realized there was going to be a flood very soon. Then panic started, and we began to save whatever we could by placing them in the loft. We kept the TV on top of the loft and moved a few more things. *Sathya* took *Ranjana* and moved to the first floor. My parents and I were on the ground floor, thinking that we could quickly move to the above shelves so they could be saved. We spent about 30 mins doing this, and then the current went off. It became pitch dark. By now, water had started to slowly enter inside our home as well. I asked my parents to move to the first floor. And then I locked the door and moved to the first floor. The whole street and neighborhood people were in panic, trying to make sense and save stuff as much as they could.

The roads submerged near our home during the floods. The black rectangle seen near the middle of the right edge is the top of a car

The aftermath after the flood recedes. The muck that required many days of washing

We kept watching as the water level rose in a slow manner. Around 11:30 pm, there were some police officers who were below, and they said they could rescue a few people. We now had to take a call; Sathya, Ranjana, and I could go with the police van to a safe place. After a quick discussion, we decided to take this route. We rushed to put our most important items, such as the laptop, purse, and passport, into a bag. Then, we decided to go with the police. We came down and couldn't open the gate in our home because it was locked. So we had to jump the wall ourselves. We got out, I carried Ranjana on my shoulder and Sathya came behind me. Water had reached about my knee level. And as we moved to the main road, the police said the van was even further! Now we have lost trust in these people - how long do we need to walk? We felt betrayed. A distant relative in a corner home on our street called my name. They invited us to their first-floor flat. So we made a quick decision and all three of us went to their home on the first floor. It is where we spent the entire gloomy night. There were about 10 to 15 people in that home. Their home had become a temporary relief home where many people from the street were staying. Through the night, we heard news that the water level might increase the next day. Fear and panic was in all our minds.

The whole night was very gloomy. It was dark because there was no electricity. But the community of people who gathered there made it somewhat passable. There were some ladies there who kept on talking and made us part of their conversations. They also made some food in the morning. Ranjana, who became a bit afraid because of the floods, felt tired and slept by that time. We all took a bit of a shut-eye and woke up the next morning. The water level now wasn't increasing. But it wasn't decreasing either. Some volunteers who braved the floods waded through neck-deep water in the streets. They provided some food and water to the people confined to their homes. It is thanks to their generosity that helped us survive that horrible night.

By afternoon, the water began to recede in a slow manner. In the evening, some boats ferried people from the flooded streets to higher ground. We took one such boat, then walked to a wedding hall. They had repurposed it as a relief center. We slept on the floor and the hall was filled with people who had moved from their homes. The next morning, we went to a hotel. We stayed for a few hours before moving to our home. Now the water had receded completely, but it left a world of muck and disaster in its wake. Things like furniture had become wet and destroyed. Many things had lost their form. A muddy layer covered the whole floor and even the shelves. It would take almost a month to complete the cleaning of the home and restore normalcy. I helped my parents as much as I could before traveling back to Bengaluru and then taking the flight to Berlin.

Excerpt from 'The Hindu' article published in Dec 1923 about a flood that happened hundred years back in Tirunelveli

There have been heavy floods in Thathaparai rivers for the last few days.

Besides, a few big tanks in the district have breached. Portions of Tirunelveli town, Shencottah, Kulasekarapuram, Veerapandiapuram, and Sinduponturai are 3 to 5 feet under water. The Tirunelveli bridge, Srivaikuntam, Tinnevelly, and Alwartirunagari Railway Stations have been under water for the last three days. Station records, staff quarters, and property have all been washed away. Bridges such as the Kulasekarapuram bridge were surrounded by water to the extent of about four miles on both sides.

All communications beyond Srivaikuntam have been cut off. Several telegraph posts have been washed away, and the railway lines have sunk into the mud. From Tinnevelly up to Trivandrum, the railway line is suspended. Trains are gradually extending to Kulasekarapuram and through more stretches. Kulasekarapuram and Tinnevelly may be reopened in another three days. Fortunately, no human life has up till now been reported lost. Arrangements are being made to the railway partially by motor trucks from Tinnevelly to Trivandrum and Kollam.

Floods in Tinnevelly bridges and surroundings are gradually subsiding since yesterday evening. Over five telegraph lines have been washed away, affecting Tinnevelly and Gangaikondan. It will take at least three days more to repair the main line of Tinnevelly, which has been covered with water and debris to several inches. Coach bodies, railway tracks, and bridges are washed away. One express and a goods train have also sunk. Floods are still three feet above road levels about eighteen inches above rail levels in and about Tinnevelly. The Tuticorin railway line has been completely closed by landslips and earth. The level crossing has been washed away. There is forty-five feet breach beyond Pettai Railway Station, and there have been minor breaches between Pettai and Tinnevelly.

Extensive damage has been reported from Eastern Taluks. The most relieving feature of the floods in the town is the absence of loss of life. Only five deaths have been reported till now, but persistent rumors are arriving that about two to three hundred dead bodies are found at Manamadurai and Srivaikuntam areas. If this were true, they must have been from the riverine villages. As there are no easy communications, definite information is not available. Total loss to the whole district is estimated to vary from one to two crores.

Reports from Tinnevelly mention that damages caused are irreparable. Heroic action by Mr. Sivasami Iyer, Drill Instructor of the Government Training School, with the help of some friends, saved many lives. Postal communication has been restored today.

The 2023 flood reminded me of one in my childhood. Then, I forgot about it. And to top that, there was a flood in Tirunelveli a hundred years ago in 1923, almost on the same date (December 16 - 20). After the 90s flood, I never expected another flood 21 years later when my daughter was 6. Again, we went to my grandmother's home, where we took refuge 21 years ago!

Somehow we scraped through it without any major loss of life. Of course, some things got damaged, but we managed to survive it.

Trauma 3 - the acute tenant trauma:

There was one more trauma in my childhood. This happened during my early childhood, around the time I was 4 or 5 years old.

We had rented a part of our home. It all started when some trouble brewed between their family and my parents. I remember waking up one day to high-pitched shouting. I went to the backyard and found my parents in a fight with the tenant's family. Since I was a kid, I didn't know the full details of it. Only that there was some conflict between both the families. The conflict came to its peak one day, portions of which I still remember.

On that particular day, my father was at work and my mother and we both kids were at home. The tenant was standing near the entrance of our home and my mother was a bit restless inside. I saw her getting anxious and she was afraid to go and talk to the tenant guy who was waiting outside (to talk about something?). My brother and I were little kids. We didn't know what to do. Should we go talk to the guy or wait for things to calm down? Even if we would talk, what would we talk about? My mother didn't let us go and at one point she got so anxious and out of her mind. A knife was involved and she got hurt. Blood started dripping from her forehand and she suffered at least three or four cuts. Watching her cry and getting hurt made me cry and I couldn't stop feeling bad for my mother. Somehow that day passed. Later, my father arrived. We took care of her. Then, the whole tenant issue went to court where it was resolved.

It affected my family. During the court case, we had to keep shifting between rental homes. My studies suffered. I began to struggle in many subjects in school. For any kid, such turbulence in the family usually leads to poor academic results, and I was no exception. Somehow, the issue got resolved after a few years, and we came back to our home. But the damage was done. For many years after, my mother was skeptical in allowing anyone else to rent our homes. She harbored a deep animosity for anyone who would ask to be a tenant in one of our house portions.

The impact on me was significant. For any kid, a mother being harmed causes deep trauma. She is the center of your universe and when she gets affected, you are impacted too. The impact lingers in your subconscious for a long time. It can take many years for a kid to get over it. As an adult, I can articulate this. But, as a child, I lacked the words and the skill to cope with the situation and its effects. Nor was there any psychological or mental counseling in those days. The impact of this incident on my mother, brother and I is deep and gradually over a period of time, we got over it.

There was probably some PTSD - Post Traumatic Stress Disorder - that my mother and I suffered from. It showed in some ways in my childhood and later. But even this vocabulary is something I picked up in my late 20s. So I am not sure how exactly this PTSD affected my family. After this issue got resolved, I started to excel in my academic work. Maybe it was a case of high-functioning depression or coping up with studies after the trauma? I am not sure.

So these are some of the traumas - mostly from my childhood and teenage years. I was lucky enough to get through some natural calamities like flood and some man made calamities like improvement.

6

Our Minimalistic Wedding, Being parents

Sathya: *Wedding and Home*

Nambirajan: *You marry and then you build a home?*

Sathya: *Or Home is what you create with your family?*

Nambirajan: *Yes, ideas of Home gets more concrete after you get married. Especially the first home that you buy/ rent/ build becomes even more memorable*

Sathya: *Like we got our first home after getting married*

Nambirajan: *And that also happened just after our daughter's birth*

Sathya: *Our home is where our young one grew up, crawling all over, scribbling on the walls and the waking up at odd hours*

Nambirajan: *That's a universal parental experience. I remember* *how I used to sing to make her sleep. Me and singing!*

Sathya: *But thanks to her, we decided to buy a home. Else we might have just continued renting?*

Nambirajan: *Most probably. Our wedding in 2016 and our daughter in 2017 were both important events leading to our home.*

Sathya: *Now lets share that story.*

Sathya: Our Minimalistic Wedding

As I continued to make progress with my therapy, I received an invitation from Nambi, whom I had first met at a book club, to attend a Landmark Forum session. Despite my reservations, I decided to go. Landmark Forum is a personal development course designed to help individuals achieve breakthroughs in their lives. The final day of the course is dedicated to inviting guests to experience it firsthand. Nambi, a firm believer in the forum's benefits, had found it transformative.

Although the session was crowded and didn't resonate deeply with me, it marked a turning point. Our acquaintance evolved into a deeper connection, and when Nambi proposed, I took a month to deliberate, even discussing the decision with my therapist. Around this time, I discovered his blog on Medium, as I was also a blog writer. I read his posts and admired his writing style and strong, firm voice. I believe writing style reflects, to some extent, how a person thinks.

While I was deliberating, I went on a trek to Kedarkantha in the Himalayas and took the necessary time to accept his proposal. At that time, Nambi was interning as a UI/UX designer at SAP Labs. Our six-month engagement was filled with both joy and challenges, but it ultimately solidified our decision to move forward together.

The process of involving our families was a mixed experience—neither overly smooth nor particularly difficult. We made the unconventional choice to have a minimalistic wedding, a departure from the extravagant norms of Indian weddings, where even middle-class families often spend exorbitantly, sometimes even borrowing money or going into debt. While our families suggested holding the wedding in either my hometown of *Madurai* or Nambi's in *Tirunelveli*, we insisted on having it at the Isha Yoga Centre in *Coimbatore*.

Our marriage in Linga Bhairavi temple in Isha Yoga Centre, Coimbatore

On May 19, 2016, we were married at the Linga Bhairavi temple within the yoga centre. The ceremony took place at 6:30 a.m. with just around 40 close friends and family members in attendance. We designed our own simple wedding invitations and kept the ritual uncomplicated, surrounded by the serene beauty of the mountains. With 50 lamps lit by Nambi and a simple 'mangalsutra' tying ceremony, it was a simple spartan Indian wedding. The overall expenditure for the marriage was just around ₹30,000. But it was an incredibly satisfying experience.

After the wedding, we relocated to Noida, near Delhi, where Nambi had secured a position as a designer at HeyTm. Although Bangalore was more familiar and sophisticated, Nambi was eager to experience the fintech startup environment at HeyTm, so we embraced this new chapter in Noida. My job at a GRC (Governance, Risk, Compliance) organization allowed me to work from home with occasional visits to the Bangalore office. Unfortunately, I didn't fully understand the policies related to travel and accommodation costs at the time, which led to some stressful situations, including late-night flights despite severe health issues.

After three months, I landed a job at one of the leading organizations in Noida as a senior consultant in the Quality team. Being the only South Indian in the office, I faced some language barriers, but my empathetic manager, Minakshi, made the transition smoother. My work involved redesigning HR processes and implementing Lean methodologies, which provided me with valuable experience managing large teams and complex projects.

Nambi and I traveled as much as we could during our Noida days. We enjoyed various treks in the Himalayas and a visit to Bhutan. We also embraced cooking, learning to adapt our recipes to avoid ingredients like chillies, garlic, and ginger, which had been causing health issues. I underwent surgery for a fissure, which prompted us to modify our cooking practices to exclude spicy ingredients.

Despite these adjustments, the winter months in Noida were challenging, and I found myself missing Bangalore's cosmopolitan culture. Additionally, I faced bias from a superior, Pooja, who favored native Hindi speakers, further adding to my discomfort.

During this period, we discovered that we were expecting a child. While Nambi was thrilled at the prospect of becoming a father, I struggled with the weight of impending motherhood. Advice from my gynecologist, coupled with maternity leave policies that had recently been extended to six months in India, helped me gradually come to terms with the reality.

A distressing incident occurred when I was in my second trimester. During a cab ride to work, our driver accidentally brushed against an SUV, leading to a confrontation where the SUV owner brandished a pistol. This frightening experience, coupled with the high crime rates in Noida, prompted us to reconsider our decision to stay there. Additionally, we also began exploring the idea of temporarily moving to our hometowns so Nambi's parents could care for me during my pregnancy.

Nambi soon secured a position at Treo in Bangalore, and we decided to return. I used my maternity leave early to ensure a healthier pregnancy and moved to Tirunelveli to stay with Nambi's parents for some quiet time. The transition from Noida was relatively smooth due to our minimalist lifestyle, marking the end of one chapter and the beginning of new experiences in Bangalore and parenthood.

Sathya: Motherhood

The saying that 'a child raises the parents' holds true in my experience. Motherhood transformed me profoundly, shifting my perspective to see the world through my child's eyes. Before our daughter was born, Nambi and I traveled frequently, but everything changed once she arrived.

During my pregnancy, I faced numerous physical and emotional challenges, though fortunately, there were no severe complications. We decided to spend my maternity break in Tirunelveli with my in-laws, which provided a serene, nature-filled environment. Nambi's father, a nature enthusiast, had created a beautiful garden near their home. This peaceful setting, combined with a diet rich in iron and calcium, including millets and drumstick soup, and the careful selection of the right doctor and hospital, contributed to a smooth pregnancy experience. Nambi traveled from Bangalore once a month, and being away from work stress made the pregnancy period more manageable. I used this time to read books on parenting and avoided disturbing news and substances like coffee and antibiotics. My focus was entirely on ensuring a healthy and joyful start for our child.

As the delivery approached, I became increasingly anxious. I sought information on the latest advancements in childbirth, particularly from Scandinavian countries, through friends like Deva. I was skeptical of Indian medical recommendations and learned about epidural anesthesia, which helps manage pain during labor by blocking nerve signals. In India, one epidural injection cost around ₹25,000, and delivery expenses varied widely, with normal deliveries costing about ₹1 lakh and C-sections around ₹2 lakhs, sometimes reaching up to ₹5 lakhs in places like Bangalore. Thankfully, my organization covered these expenses through health insurance, but parenting remains a costly affair in India.

On Ganesh Chaturthi 2017, my water broke in the early morning, which felt like a heavy period flow. Nambi was in Bangalore, so I went to the hospital with my anxious in-laws. After eight hours of labor with an epidural, I underwent a C-section. This major surgery involves a horizontal incision below the stomach to deliver the baby. Our daughter was born at 6:20 p.m. on a Friday. Post-surgery, I experienced severe pain and difficulty moving from the bed. I am grateful to my relatives who supported me through sleepless nights until I could walk on my own. The physical recovery took a month, with continuous bleeding and significant discomfort.

The first year of motherhood was a steep learning curve. The initial month after delivery is crucial and filled with sleepless nights, as newborns are often awake during the night. It's ideal to have additional support to manage night shifts. The first 45 days are particularly challenging, with heightened susceptibility to illness and heavy sweating. Postpartum depression and conflicts with family members added to the stress. I came to understand the saying, 'It takes a village to raise a child,' as even with four people at home, managing a newborn was exhausting.

Sleep became incredibly valuable, and I learned the importance of setting boundaries in relationships to maintain mental health. We decided to move to Bangalore from Tirunelveli, and with our minimalistic lifestyle, we managed to purchase our first flat within our budget and planned to repay the loan within 5 to 10 years.

Reflecting on this period, I wish I had sought postpartum

counseling with a therapist. It would have been beneficial to address mood swings and physical discomfort more effectively. Regular check-ups that include monitoring vitamin levels like Vitamin D and Vitamin B12, along with physiotherapy for back and cervical pain, could have improved my recovery.

After settling into our new home in Bangalore, Nambi's startup faced layoffs due to poor traction and sales. This unexpected turn was alarming, especially since Nambi was the primary breadwinner at that time. I took a career break until our daughter turned one, while Nambi dealt with health issues related to bladder stones caused by inadequate water intake during his time in a PG accommodation. With a significant loan and parenting responsibilities, I began job hunting again. My friend Priya Sundaram referred me to job openings within a 5 km radius from home, which was crucial for balancing work and family life. Prioritizing job stability over salary, I focused on finding a well-established organization. Priya's guidance helped me navigate the negotiation process, and I secured a position as a Senior Consultant with a package of ₹12.5 lakhs per annum. This was a significant relief for us since we no longer had to depend on one person for managing the family expenses.

By this time, Nambi had also secured a job at Walmart. With both of us working, a new baby, and a new home, we finally felt relieved. We had overcome the financial struggles of our early career days and found great places to work and grow together. It felt like we had finally found our home and settled in Bengaluru for good.

Nambirajan: On Fatherhood and a few realizations

I first met Sathya during a book club meeting in Bengaluru. I was studying at NID, and after co-founding the 'We Read Therefore We Are' book club in Chennai, I decided to start a chapter in Bengaluru. Sathya attended one of our meetups, and while we became Facebook friends, I quickly forgot about her. Later, while studying at NID, I was involved in the ILP program, which included inviting friends to Landmark programs. Most people I reached out to didn't show up, but Sathya did. This rekindled our acquaintance, and I invited her to visit the NID campus in Peenya, Bengaluru.

Our relationship began to blossom, with frequent meetings before my semester exchange in Zurich. One memorable conversation was about the Himalayas. I was cautious about sharing my upcoming Zurich semester exchange and told her I was going to a place like the Himalayas and needed winter clothing. She recommended Decathlon, which at the time didn't impress me, leading to some messages of frustration on my part. Despite this, we stayed in touch through Skype calls and messages during my time in Zurich. When I returned to India, our relationship deepened, and by the time I joined HeyTm, it had become serious.

The decision to marry Sathya was straightforward for me. She loved me deeply, and what more reason do you need to marry someone who loves you that much? As people, we seemed to have different interests and hobbies, and even different political views. One incident during our dating days highlights this. We attended a standup comedy event at Jagriti Theater in Bengaluru. The comedian's set veered into the Tamil language, and she asked the audience if anyone spoke Tamil. We both raised our hands. She then asked, "Do you believe Tamil is older than Sanskrit?" Spontaneously, I said "Yes," and Sathya said "No." This drew laughter from the audience and underscored our differing perspectives, even on cultural topics.

At some point in our relationship, I had to make a decision. I knew I liked her, but I wasn't sure if she was the person I wanted to marry. Rather than over analyze, I decided to move forward. I met her father in Bengaluru and arranged for my family to visit hers in Madurai. We decided to marry at the Isha Linga Bhairavi Temple in Coimbatore, despite initial resistance from both families. The wedding date was set for May 19, 2016, coinciding with the Tamil Nadu state elections, making the week even more memorable.

We got engaged in January 2016 and had a simple wedding in May, attended by around 50 people from both families. None of my friends could make it, but Sathya's friends were present. The ceremony was simple and held in the auspicious presence of the Linga Bhairavi Temple.

After getting married, we moved to Noida since I was working at HeyTm. Although we didn't have many friends there, we created a small circle of acquaintances. One notable connection was Rajakrishnan, a childhood friend from Tirunelveli who was now an art faculty member at an international school in Noida. It was heartwarming to reconnect with someone from my early days.

Life in Noida wasn't without challenges. Sathya and I often fought over trivial matters but would always reconcile. We also went on memorable treks, including trips to Prashar Lake and Kheerganga. Camping amidst lush green mountains and by serene lakes remains etched in my memory. While the Prashar Lake trek was peaceful, the Kheerganga trek was marked by incessant rain during our descent, making it both challenging and unforgettable.

Work at HeyTm presented its own difficulties. The culture was highly competitive and aggressive, with little collaboration or camaraderie among colleagues. As part of the design team, we conducted research related to HeyTm's QR-based payment system, including user interviews with rickshaw drivers and shop owners. However, the lack of mentorship and support made it a toxic workplace. By 2015, terms like 'toxic work culture' weren't widely used, but HeyTm epitomized the concept with its poor communication, lack of respect, and negative atmosphere. Within a year, I knew I needed to find a new job.

This period coincided with Sathya's pregnancy, adding another layer of stress. Balancing job hunting with supporting Sathya was challenging. An interview at a pharma-tech company in Gurgaon backfired when the interviewer informed my manager at HeyTm, worsening the workplace environment for me. I accelerated my job search and secured a position at a Bengaluru startup focused on building microservices for underserved communities in India.

Meanwhile, Sathya moved to my hometown, Tirunelveli, for her delivery, where my parents could care for her. Our daughter,

Ranjana, was born on August 25, 2017. Soon after, minor conflicts arose between my mother and Sathya's family, prompting us to move to Madurai temporarily. In February 2018, we bought a home in Bengaluru and relocated there, marking the beginning of a new chapter in our lives.

Celebrating Ranjana's first birthday in our new home in Bengaluru

From February 2018 to May 2022, Ranjana grew up in Bengaluru, where I was working at Walmart, and Sathya joined her new job at Infotech (name changed). Since we were both juggling demanding careers, we sought the help of Rani akka, a kind woman from Madurai. She became an invaluable part of our daily life, managing cooking, cleaning, and most importantly, caring for Ranjana in our absence.

However, we made a mistake by giving Rani akka a mobile phone to show kids' videos to Ranjana. What started as a harmless distraction quickly turned into an unhealthy habit. Ranjana became glued to the screen, spending hours watching those relentless Cocomelon videos. At one point, we even found ourselves watching them with her on TV, bemused by their strangely hypnotic appeal.

One day while working at Walmart, I checked my home webcam and it was disheartening to see Ranjana engrossed in the mobile screen and Rani akka watching the TV. I realized we were not spending enough time with our kid, focusing more on our work. We sought some support from my parents to help raise Ranjana. Unfortunately, tensions between Sathya and my mother during visits also limited the involvement of my family in Ranjana's care. Eventually, we had to continue with a nanny for additional support.

The Covid pandemic brought an unexpected pause to this dynamic. Starting in February 2020, the lockdowns confined us to our home, giving us more time to bond with Ranjana. In hindsight, those two years became a pivotal period in our parenting journey. I realize now that I wasn't as involved in Ranjana's emotional and social development as I could have been during her early years. Despite spending evenings with her, I often found my efforts weren't enough.

The lockdown, however, gave us the chance to correct course. It was a blessing in disguise. We gradually weaned Ranjana off the mobile phone—a small victory—only to face a new challenge: the iPad. Though we've become stricter about her screen time and closely ration the minutes she spends watching videos, the allure of YouTube Kids remains strong. I often feel a tinge of regret knowing we inadvertently contributed to raising one of the 'iPad kids' of her generation.

Since moving to Germany, I've been able to spend even more time with Ranjana. Here, there's a wealth of opportunities for her, including free Museum Sundays where many museums open their doors to the public on the first Sunday of every month. A healthier work-life balance allows us to encourage her participation in music and ballet classes, which she thoroughly enjoys.

Looking back, raising Ranjana has been a journey filled with ups and downs. We weren't perfect parents by any measure, and I deeply relate to the struggles of working parents everywhere. The challenge of balancing careers while nurturing a young child is immense, and mistakes are inevitable. Yet, through these mistakes, we grew—both as individuals and as parents. It's a journey of learning, love, and resilience, and one I wouldn't trade for anything.

7

Balancing Act - Balancing work and family

Sathya: *I have a lot to say on this topic being a mother*

Nambirajan: *I can imagine. And some of it will be complaints against me?*

Sathya: *Haha, complaints are never ending. More than that it's about how both of us can manage our work and also our families. I guess we both sacrificed in our one ways for our family*

Nambirajan: *Yes, you came out of the workforce for about 6 months after our daughter was born. And even while working in Infotech, you took part time work for a few months to balance both home and work responsibilities.*

Sathya: *And you...*

Nambirajan: *What did I do?*

Sathya: *You *did* support me - coming from work early at 4 pm to take care of Ranjana and then dropping a fat paycheck offer in India and choosing to work in Germany*

Nambirajan: *I would have been a Director of Design if... (sigh)*

Sathya: *All the ifs and buts of life. Let's start our chapter*

Sathya: Resuming My Work Life

I joined my current organization on June 18, 2018, and it felt like I was reclaiming my own time. Work became a form of therapy during that period, providing me with much-needed structure and routine. Having spent the last nine months at home caring for my daughter, I had even stopped dressing up, focusing entirely on her. Returning to the office brought a sense of normalcy, and I was fortunate to have my friend Priya on the same team. She made me feel comfortable in every aspect, easing my transition back to work. I also made new friends at the office, many of whom were fellow mothers. Sharing our struggles created a sense of camaraderie, and I was grateful for the strong senior buddy network. One of those connections, in particular, continues to be a joyful part of my life today.

However, as I hadn't weaned my daughter yet, there were some discomforts during office hours. Like many working mothers, I managed with breast pads and pumps, and within six months, things eased up once breastfeeding was over. Around that time, Nambi secured a job as a UI designer at Walmart Labs, and his health improved. We juggled our work schedules with support from my in-laws, and we got through the year together.

Our family operates on a simple principle: we share everything—household chores, finances, and responsibilities. When one of us faces challenges, the other steps up. We also keep our financial needs minimal, thinking carefully before purchasing anything unnecessary. One guiding rule in our home is to maintain open spaces and avoid clutter. We've always kept our living space simple, with functional furniture, and we've never owned a car or fancy gadgets. Our home evolved along with our daughter. We left plenty of space for her to crawl and play, even sleeping on mattresses on the floor to make life simpler. As the saying goes, "Jealousy comes from comparison." We avoid this by living below our means and using our savings for experiences, not material upgrades. This approach gives us peace of mind, knowing we have enough savings to manage for a year if either of us lose our job.

As time passed, my in-laws became fatigued from caring for a small child all day, so we decided to bring in a full-time nanny from my hometown, Madurai. I had saved enough to afford her, and we hired Rani Akka, an experienced caregiver and a fantastic cook. She stayed with us for a year, establishing a routine with Ranjana and preparing delicious meals. Nambi would come home around 3 pm to take over, and I would be back by 5:15 pm to continue the handover. We avoided taking on high-responsibility office work during that time. My boss and team knew that I wouldn't be available after 5 pm. To me, parenting is one of the most heroic acts in the world. If we can be fully involved in our child's life, especially until they turn seven, we can help shape their personality in the best way. My in-laws continued to support us when they could, and we managed until Ranjana turned three.

During this time, I was performing well at work and had great mentors. But then, in 2021, the COVID-19 pandemic hit, disrupting work for everyone, especially in the IT sector. Most of us started working from home, which was challenging at first, especially with a two-year-old, but we eventually adapted, as did the organization. There were moments when the workload felt overwhelming. My manager, Karthikeyan, was an incredible mentor who truly cared about his team. There were times I considered quitting due to the stress of balancing work and motherhood, but Karthik encouraged me to explore part-time work options instead. I read up on the company's policy and decided to take it. In well-established organizations, such supportive policies are invaluable. I worked part-time for three months, which allowed me to spend more time with Ranjana in the afternoons. During this time, my work hours and pay were halved, but it was a blessing.

COVID made work life somewhat monotonous without the office buddy system. That's when I considered changing jobs. However, Karthik advised me to be patient, assuring me that better opportunities would arise within the same organization. His support was instrumental, and he played a pivotal role in my current position in Germany. I stopped thinking about switching jobs just to keep up with the rat race and instead focused on doing my best work. One of the smartest things I did for myself was self-sponsoring an annual certification in my field. Sadly, we lost Karthik and his family in a tragic car accident near Trichy, and only his daughter survived. The incident reminded me of the accident my own family experienced near Trichy a decade ago. It took me a while to come to terms with the loss.

At home, Nambi and I grew tired of the monotony of sitting indoors during the lockdown, so we decided to start a YouTube channel together, called 'Sathya Nambirajan.' We made videos on a wide various topics, from book reviews to quiz games, without much clarity about our niche at first. Eventually, the channel found its focus on sharing about our life experiences in Germany. COVID also gave birth to my gardening hobby, which brought me great joy.

As Ranjana turned three, we wanted someone who could engage with her and help instill good habits. We found a kindergarten teacher, Kalpana, who had lost her job due to the pandemic, and she became our new daytime nanny. She was a tremendous help, and without her support and Rani Akka's contributions, it would have been much harder to manage. Nambi even booked Rani Akka a flight ticket as a token of our appreciation, as the borders were closed and flights were her only option to return to Madurai. She was thrilled about her first flight experience.

By then, we were also exploring job opportunities abroad, particularly in Europe, with Germany as our top choice. The reasons were clear: quality education for our daughter, safety for women, and the opportunity to travel across Europe while we were still young. I wasn't keen on the U.S., as it seemed too competitive with poor work-life balance and lenient gun laws. Nambi took the first step, but the recruitment process in

Germany was slow. After two rejections and a year of waiting, he finally received an offer from a company in Berlin. Meanwhile, my organization also offered me an onsite opportunity in Germany. Patience and joyful work opened doors for us.

We both started learning German while still in Bangalore, knowing it would be essential for life in Germany. English wouldn't suffice. The visa process took time, and while Nambi moved to Berlin in February 2022, my daughter and I had to wait three more months for our visas. During those months, I managed with help from Kalpana, a day care teacher, while dealing with my office work, visa procedures, bank matters, packing, and preparing our home for tenants. The stress took a toll on me, and in the final week before our flight, my daughter got food poisoning from french fries in a Bengaluru restaurant. I'm incredibly grateful to Priya and Kalpana, who stood by me in the emergency ward, taking care of my daughter. We stayed at Priya's home as we recovered, though the stress remained heavy on me.

When the time came to fly, Nambi had finally found us a place in Berlin. My daughter and I flew alone, navigating a 12-hour journey with a layover in Qatar. It was a midnight flight, and Priya and her family came to send us off at the airport. Saying goodbye to my close friends and family, who had supported me so much, was difficult. But I've always believed in the power of the right support network, especially among women, and it's that network that helped me tackle these challenges.

Nambirajan: Continuing my journey further

To be honest, I didn't have much struggle in managing my family and career. As a man, I had the privilege of choosing my career paths irrespective of where I was in my family - raising journey. I started working in a new city—Noida—after I got married, and my wife adapted to it. It was my choice, primarily, to move to North India, and thanks to my wife's willingness to move and try it out, the choice became easier. In hindsight, it was a mistake since things didn't pan out the way we had hoped. And we both had to bear the consequences of the mistake. We also had to move again, this time back to Bengaluru. Sathya could have chosen not to come with me to Noida. But she chose to come with me to Noida, and again later, when I decided to move to Berlin for work, she chose to come with me again. Though coming to Berlin might have been a mutually beneficial call, the move to Noida was definitely a sacrifice she made for me.

Looking back from a gender perspective, it's the women in our lives who make career pauses during childbirth and raising children, and then rejoin the workforce. Men like me have had it good. We continue with our careers almost unscathed by marriage or childbirth. So if I had to say anything about how I struggled to manage work and family, I would be lying. At the same time, like many fathers I also had my own emotional journey as a father. But those are minuscule in comparison to the challenges women face as mothers and to balance work and family. So let me take this chance, and a few pages here, to continue my life story sharing instead some of my challenges in the work front.

After the mistakes of *HeyTm*, I joined Trio, determined to make it work. Trio had its office in HSR Layout, and I found a small shared rental room in HSR. The walk from home to office could be done in less than 20 minutes, and in the traffic-congested streets of Bengaluru, that was a blessing. Trio was taking a unique approach to build a set of services like booking bus tickets, checking train status, or paying utility bills using the USSD platform, which is used in basic phones to transfer information between the phone and network. For example, dialing *123# to check your balance actually happens on the USSD platform. To borrow a commonly used information tech analogy, it was like a lesser-used service road for the heavily congested information superhighway that is broadband internet.

Now, with the benefit of hindsight, it was a startup born dead because Jio, which had launched a few years earlier, was rapidly building inroads into the telecom industry, acquiring users by the millions from every stratum of the Indian consumer base. But when I was working at Trio, we continued to work on our ideas, designing and building services on the USSD platform. I worked on a few features like the onboarding flow for UPI and bill payment microservices. UPI was the new tech kid on the block, with many fintech platforms racing to build payment platforms using UPI.

All was well until about December 2018—we even got acquired by Hike. The overall plan was to integrate the Hike wallet with Trio's microservices and make Hike a super app. There were plans for billions of rupees being transacted on Hike. But just two months later, things flipped. Hike dropped the plan to implement payment microservices and abandoned the super app route. Aspirations of billions of rupees being transacted—all vaporized quickly—and a real existential threat began for most of the team. Years later, Hike would close its messenger and focus on a few game-based apps. But the beginning of this end had just happened. This again meant I had to find new work, a new team, a new mission to work toward. Again, the job search started.

Maybe it was the job market, or I wasn't looking in the right places, but I struggled to find work in those days. I finally scraped together a job at a startup in Whitefield with a big pay cut. But with a home loan payment due every month, I needed to find something good and quick. I continued my job search and finally found work at Walmart Labs, which had set up a design team in its development center near Bellandur, Bengaluru. Thanks to a referral from an NID senior who was working there, I got an opportunity to interview with them. There was an assignment about 'Scan and Go' during the interview process—a feature in which users can scan items directly on their phones and pay for them through the phone. This eliminated the need to wait in checkout queues. I believe I did fairly well in the assignment, and the other interviews went well too. Finally, I landed a role in the design team at Walmart Labs. A new chapter in my work life began.

After having a couple of work misfires with first *HeyTm* and later Trio, I decided to put my best efforts into making my work at Walmart successful. I started putting focused efforts at work, and in a year or so, it began to pay dividends. I was working in their International team, which was building applications for the Walmart brands in Mexico. I was working specifically to design features for Sam's Club, a membership-based brand in Mexico. Their existing Android and iOS apps were riddled with inconsistencies and archaic patterns and needed an uplift—a redesign to provide a better user experience. That was one of the good works I did in my stint at Walmart Labs.

It was during this time that I got an opportunity to travel to Mexico. There was a set of usability tests planned in Mexico City, where we were to test some of the redesigns we had just completed. Along with completing the tests, we were also planning to travel to San Francisco to the Walmart office in Sunnyvale. It was my first travel experience with respect to my design work outside India, and I was excited about it.

Visiting the Teotihuacan pyramids in Mexico City

Working on Sam's Club Mexico projects also meant we got exposure to the Spanish language, a few words of which I learned from the Duolingo app. '*Como se siente*' (How are you?) is one such phrase that I learned during this time. The usability tests in Mexico went well. One learning from this was how some of the icons we assumed people would understand turned out to be indecipherable or even misunderstood. After the visit to Mexico and then to Walmart HQ in Sunnyvale, we returned to India.

Again, I would get an opportunity to travel to Mexico the following year. This time, we focused more on visiting the Sam's Club stores in Mexico City than on office work. We realized that getting acquainted with the actual working of the stores was as important as completing desk tasks. During this visit, along with completing our tasks, we also utilized some free time to visit the Teotihuacan pyramids near Mexico City, an ancient site from Mayan civilization.

Unlike the previous year, this time I took a week's break after completing both the Mexico and San Francisco legs of the trip. I visited New York and spent a few days traveling around the city. This was February 2019. The early signs of the Covid pandemic had just started to show up. But as a traveler in New York, I wasn't fully aware of the signs of this coming wave. One thing I was aware of, though, was that after completing a city walk (where one of the walkers kept sneezing), I woke up the next day and coughed up a concerning amount of blood. I didn't realize it could have been Covid. I just brushed it off as a random occurrence and moved on. Later, when my flight landed, things got strange. People on my flight were asked to fill out forms about our health conditions and addresses. I didn't know at the time, but the Indian government was trying to quarantine people coming from abroad in an effort to control the spread of the pandemic. Later, I also found a sheet containing all the addresses of people who had traveled abroad and landed in Bengaluru leaked online – that's the kind of information privacy that exists.

My company enforced a mandatory Work From Home for all its employees, and a few days later, the Prime Minister of India came on TV and announced a nationwide lockdown. What started with a single person expanded to the entire company, and now the entire country was in lockdown. The virus was rampaging, filling hospital beds, and killing millions of people around the world. Companies struggled to adapt to this new kind of work where people wouldn't come to the office at all. Work From Home became the new normal. Successive waves of Covid would wreak even more harm. Confusion related to vaccine efficacy would create its own chaos. In the midst of all this, many people struggled to continue their livelihoods. Millions of poor migrants in India walked hundreds of miles to their hometowns since bus and train services were stopped. The entire impact of Covid cannot be captured in this paragraph, but it was a crisis of immense proportions wrought upon the entire world.

By the beginning of 2021, things slowly started to return to normal. Vaccination rates improved, and the virus began to recede. Just as Covid was receding, my work at Walmart was also slowing down. Changes in management and their aftermath led to a new hybrid team emerging. All good things come to an end. After again being overlooked for a promotion, I decided to make a move to a new company.

Looking back, joining Walmart as a Product Designer marked a significant improvement in my career. Working with the International team introduced me to a multicultural work environment. My role also allowed me to visit Walmart's offices in Sunnyvale and Mexico City. This period, from 2018 to 2020, was a high point in my career, offering structured critique and collaborative work within a diverse, multilingual design team. The opportunity to conduct usability tests, an often-overlooked aspect of design, was particularly fulfilling.

As I reflect on these past experiences, I see a journey filled with challenges, unexpected turns, and valuable lessons. My career has taken me from the competitive environment of *HeyTm*, through the ups and downs at Trio and Walmart, to the exciting new chapter in Berlin. In the next chapter, I'll delve into the decision to move to Germany, share my experiences in Berlin, and explore the many transitions that have shaped my career.

8

Berlin Beginnings - Our initial years in Germany

Sathya: *So when did we decide to move to Germany?*

Nambirajan: *It was many years in the making. My interest started with my semester exchange in Germany in 2015. Before we wanted to move to Germany, remember which country we were thinking and planning for?*

Sathya: *Canada*

Nambirajan: *Yes, in spite of making some efforts Canada never came through. And Covid gave us enough time to reflect*

Sathya: *And in one of those conversations we discussed about moving to Europe and then you started applying*

Nambirajan: *I applied for more than 100 companies in Stepstone. Most got rejected. Even in Texad I got rejected.*

Sathya: *Then we had a turnaround*

Nambirajan: *Texad came back and gave me a job offer*

Sathya: *With that we made the move to Berlin*

Sathya: Our move to Germany

Ranjana and I landed at Berlin Brandenburg Airport after a 12-hour journey. Throughout the flight, my daughter kept asking for her father, eager to reunite with Nambi. The stress of the trip triggered my period, making it even harder to cope during the flight. I couldn't leave my daughter alone, so I avoided using the restroom. Looking back, I realize I should've asked the flight crew for help, but stress clouded my judgment. After clearing customs, we stepped into Berlin, where everything around us switched to German. Even connecting to Wi-Fi was challenging since all the web pages were in German. We faced some struggles until we finally reached Nambi, who had been waiting for us. Thankfully, I had packed light, which made it easier to manage both our luggage and my daughter.

Ranjana was overjoyed to see her father after three months. My stress melted away in that moment. Nambi had his own share of struggles—he had applied for over 30 apartments in vain before securing a six-month rental contract. In Germany, contracts are strictly adhered to, down to the last word.

The first few weeks were wonderful. We arrived in spring, and Berlin's gardens and walking paths were filled with vibrant blossoms. But the initial euphoria soon gave way to reality. Navigating German processes was overwhelming—everything from securing a spot in kindergarten (called *Kita* in German) to registering our home address at the *Bürgeramt*. On top of that, my work started almost immediately. It took six months for us to truly grasp the 'do-it-yourself' culture that prevails in Germany. The language barrier was the hardest part. Public offices, visa offices, and schools all communicated primarily in German, and our A1-level German wasn't enough to understand.

During our first year of stay in Germany, there were moments when I just wanted to cry—whether during office calls or while trying to pay bills that arrived too late by mail. Fines for late payments piled up because we couldn't keep up with the slow postal system. It took us more than six months to figure out how everything worked.

During those tough first few months, Nambi even had to undergo hernia surgery from lifting heavy items. We didn't have close friends yet, just a few acquaintances, so we navigated everything alone. It was hard. We seriously considered returning to India. I even had to visit the gynecologist multiple times due to stress-related health issues, and the language barrier made it difficult to book appointments. One common perception of German doctors is that they often say, 'You are okay. Just have hot water and play sport/take a walk,' for many health issues. The doctors we met had a similar attitude—after a few checkups, all they could tell me was to 'accept your body.' Looked another way it was a welcome change from the antibiotics filled prescriptions given by Indian doctors.

We decided to give ourselves a year before making any big decisions. That's when we started documenting our experiences on our YouTube channel. It became a creative outlet, a lifeline. Slowly, we began to make friends in the expat community. We met three South Indian families at a lake, and Ranjana found her first friend, Pavani (name changed). Pavani's family even helped us find a long-term rental apartment, a significant milestone since housing in Berlin is incredibly competitive. Most German apartment owners prefer European tenants, and many immigrants from India struggle to find apartments in Berlin.

As we settled into our new home, our neighborhood became more familiar. Ranjana made friends, and I started connecting with other mothers. The sense of belonging grew, but it took a year to get there. Winters in Berlin were especially tough—dark, cold, and lonely. But Nambi had an idea: he began organizing meetups for newcomers to Berlin, which helped others find their footing and made life a bit easier.

By the end of our first year, we had adapted to the German way of life. I resumed my German classes and aimed to complete my B1 level. After failing my A1 exam on the first try—due to a series of mistakes like missing my train and arriving late—I worked hard with a private tutor. I finally passed B1 after a year and a half. Learning the language changed everything. I could read grocery labels, communicate in public spaces, and began to understand and accept German culture.

We also discovered some joyful and supportive moments amidst the struggles. Through a Facebook group, we received free furniture from a kindhearted person, Elni, who later became a family friend. The German government's generous child support and free public transport for kids under six were also blessings during this time.

The first few months in Berlin were a rollercoaster, but every struggle shaped our story. If you are planning, thinking, or wondering about coming to Germany, know that the first year of living here might be the toughest.

Nambirajan: From Bengaluru to Berlin — First Year in Berlin

When I transitioned from Walmart to FinMobi, India's design market was thriving. This was just after the COVID-19 pandemic, and there was a significant rise in salaries offered for tech roles in Bengaluru. During my time at FinMobi, working on live commerce for Roposo and Glance's integration with Google, I began interviewing with various brands. Ola, Redbus, and PhonePe were some of the notable companies that reached the final stages of discussions.

Ola's process reached the offer stage but then went silent for weeks, which frustrated me. I had also heard less-than-favorable things about Ola's work culture. PhonePe advanced to the final rounds but didn't lead to an offer. Redbus extended a lucrative offer with the title of Associate Director of Design, which would have been a big leap in my career, but it came a little too late. Around the same time as the Redbus offer, I received an offer from a German company, Texad.

Having applied to hundreds of European companies and faced countless rejections, Texad's offer was a welcome change. I started seriously considering moving to Germany to work as a product designer. Although I hadn't heard of Texad before, they were a service company based in Germany, working on projects for FolksHagen (name changed). Their website wasn't impressive, but they were the only company that responded positively. After completing their interview process, including a task assignment, I waited for weeks without any updates. By November 2022, Texad re-engaged, and within weeks, I had my visa and ticket ready. I was set to start at Texad on February 14, 2023.

During my semester exchange in Zurich years ago, I had dreamt of working as a designer in Europe. My student budget back then had limited my ability to experience the continent fully. Seven years later, that dream was finally becoming a reality. On February 12, 2023, I flew from Bengaluru to Frankfurt and then took a train to Wolfsburg, where Texad was headquartered. One small culture shock I experienced on the train from Berlin to Wolfsburg was the complete silence. Coming from India, where train rides are filled with chatter and noise, the quietness was strange, almost unsettling.

Wolfsburg was an interesting first stop. As FolksHagen's headquarters and Texad's base, it was a city centered around the automotive industry. My first days, however, were spent in quarantine due to Germany's COVID-19 protocols. Because India was classified as a 'red zone,' I needed additional vaccinations. Having already taken Covaxin in India, I believed I was vaccinated enough. But Germany had its own vaccine rules simply called as 3G (*Geimpft, Genesen, Getestet* which roughly translates to 'Vaccinated, Recovered, Tested'). I learnt that Covaxxin wasn't recognized in Germany, I had to receive two doses of Moderna as well. With a total of four vaccinations, I joked that I was probably immune to COVID for the next 40 years.

Wolfsburg is truly FolksHagen's city. The massive factory produces millions of cars annually, and numerous companies in the area are tied to FolksHagen in some capacity. Texad, where I joined as part of their team, had grown from a single project for FolksHagen to a company with over 200 employees and multimillion-Euro projects. Though I moved to Berlin within 10 days, I would return to Wolfsburg often for events, conferences, and team meetings. If you're connected to FolksHagen, Wolfsburg is the center of that universe.

At Texad, I began working on Heartbeat, a software status tracking tool. I got to know more about my team and the project slowly. One missed opportunity during my time in Wolfsburg was attending a football match at the city's stadium. Texad had a corporate box with tickets available, but my quarantine prevented me from attending this. To this day, I haven't watched a match there.

On February 26, 2023, just days after arriving in Germany, I moved to Berlin. The date is etched in my memory because it coincided with the start of the Russia-Ukraine war. The war profoundly impacted Europe, with Berlin witnessing a significant influx of Ukrainian refugees. It also worsened Berlin's housing crisis, which became a personal challenge for me. Even as I write this, around 1,000 days later, the war rages on. Cities in Ukraine have been reduced to rubble, and recovery will be an uphill struggle. With the recent victory of Trump in the US elections, there's talk that the war might end with a victory for Russia—an unfortunate and farcical conclusion.

Berlin came with its own culture shocks. One of the first things I noticed was the silence on public transportation. Even dogs here are calm and quiet, and the crows barely caw, unlike their noisy counterparts in India. Another quirk was the German approach to breakfast. Unlike in southern *Tamil Nadu* where steaming hot meals are a cultural staple, cold food is commonly eaten here. I survived those first months in Berlin with my limited cooking skills.

One negative experience during my initial days in Berlin was getting fined for traveling without a bus ticket. I was in a rush to attend a session by Sadhguru and thought I'd buy the monthly pass the next day. Unfortunately, a ticket inspector showed up, and I was fined 60 Euros. Delaying payment increased the fine to 100 Euros. When I went to the BVG office to settle it, the attendant refused to speak English, turning the situation into a nightmare. While I understand the fine, a bit more empathy would have gone a long way.

However, this paled in comparison to the challenge of finding a house in Berlin. Germany's rental market is aggressive and competitive. Landlords prefer German residents, making it tough for newcomers. Apartment hunting involved filling lengthy applications on platforms like Immoscout and attending viewings, sometimes alongside hundreds of others. Despite numerous applications, I struggled to get appointments. With my family set to join me in a few months, the clock was ticking.

A chance encounter at a railway station led me to UG, a platform that offered me an apartment in Lankwitz. Though the rent was steep at 1,300 Euros, I had no better options and signed a seven-month lease. In May, Sathya and Ranjana joined me in Berlin. The first six months were challenging, from navigating the healthcare system to finding a Kita (childcare) for Ranjana. Initially we stayed in Lankwitz, a leafy neighborhood in southern Berlin. Though we had a few helpful neighbors, the overall experience was that of isolation and detachment from the community. We felt isolated in our struggles, but eventually, things improved. By November, a friend referred us to a more affordable apartment near a serene lake, which made things better.

Learning German has been another uphill task. While I had completed an A1 course in India during the pandemic, it was barely enough for daily life in Berlin. My wife, who needed B1 certification for her job, cleared her exams after some initial struggles. I managed to pass my A1 exam as well, but mastering the language requires years of consistent effort. German grammar, with its gendered nouns and complex rules, is particularly challenging.

Socially, building connections in Germany takes time. Unlike

India, where hospitality and friendship come easily, forming relationships here can take years. Germans don't readily invite newcomers into their lives. For example, when we sought help finding a hospital for our daughter, the Kita staff directed us to a random facility without pediatric services. After several wrong turns, we finally found the right one ourselves. The apartment hunt was no different - we had to navigate that journey entirely by ourselves. If you're moving to Germany, adopt a DIY (do-it-yourself) mindset—don't expect help to come easily.

Raising Ranjana in Germany has had its ups and downs. While Kita applications were initially overwhelming, we eventually secured a spot. Though commuting two hours daily to drop and pick her up was tough, Ranjana adjusted well. She began picking up German quickly from her classmates and teachers, adapting to her new environment better than we expected.

*Ranjana with the '**Schultüte**' - a German tradition where they provide school supplies in a cone during the beginning of an academic year*

One integral part of an immigrant's experience, especially during the first few years, is navigating cultural differences. Germany offers its fair share of quirks that can leave newcomers amused, confused, or outright baffled. Take breakfast, for instance—some Germans prefer to eat first and then brush their teeth. It's a small but unexpected twist for many of us who do things the other way around.

Walking holds a special place in German life. It's not just exercise; it's a way to bond, relax, or celebrate. Whether it's a casual date, a family outing, or part of holiday traditions, walking seems to be a universal answer for everything. Equally surprising is the eerie calm of Sundays when stores close entirely. For someone from India, where markets bustle every day of the week, this quiet takes some getting used to. It also means you'll need to plan your weekend shopping carefully.

Then there's the sparkling water dilemma. Germans often prefer sparkling water over still water, a choice that initially puzzled me. 'What in heaven is sparkling water?' was my first reaction. Over time, I've come to see it as part of their taste for things with a fizzy twist, but it's definitely an acquired preference. Personally for me, I am firmly in the *'ohne kohlensaure'* camp - preferring to drink water without carbonation.

German efficiency shines through in their habit of planning. Holidays, for instance, are mapped out well in advance—sometimes a year or more. It's a level of organization that's admirable but can be intimidating for those of us accustomed to more spontaneous plans. In comparison, we Indians plan holidays usually just a month in advance.

Winters in Germany can be especially tough for immigrants, not just because of the biting cold but also due to loneliness. With temperatures dropping below 10 degrees and few friends around, the long, dark evenings can feel isolating. To combat this, I started ***Cricket Konnect***—a cricket club where we met every Sunday at Tempelhof Stadium to play cricket during the summer of 2022. The sheer novelty of playing cricket in the heart of Berlin brought together desi guys from all walks of life, creating a vibrant and connected community. Even now, we continue to play cricket every summer in Tempelhof.

Of course, cricket isn't practical year-round, especially with harsh winters. To keep the community spirit alive, I extended the idea to form ***Culture Konnect***—a meetup group where people gather at restaurants to enjoy good food and great conversations. This initiative was an instant hit. Our first Indian meetup received over 150 RSVPs, and around 40 people showed up, proving there was a real demand for spaces where people could meet, share stories, and form connections.

Since then, we've hosted these meetups almost every month, consistently drawing a warm and enthusiastic crowd. We even welcomed participants from other countries occasionally, making it an enriching cultural exchange. I'll share the QR code for our meetup page so that if you're in Germany or planning to move here, you can join us for a Culture Konnect event. It's been a joy building this community, knowing it helps people beat the loneliness and find a sense of belonging.

And then there are the biggest cultural shocks—those moments that leave you staring in disbelief. Public displays of affection are entirely normal here, a sharp contrast to the more restrained norms back home. Even more shocking? Nudity in saunas is considered completely normal. It's part of a relaxed, open-minded approach to life that can take a while to wrap your head around.

Immigration isn't just about moving to a new place; it's about adapting to a new way of life. From understanding quirky traditions to building a support system, every experience shapes your journey in unique ways.

Herbst/ Autumn time in Berlin where we experienced all four seasons for the first time

After relocating within Berlin, our life took a significant turn for the better. We found a much-improved Kita for Ranjana, ensuring she was happy and well cared for. The community in our new apartment complex was incredibly welcoming, with several Indian families who made the transition feel a lot less isolating. Weekends became something to look forward to, as we gathered to play cricket, strengthening bonds and creating a fun routine.

By this time, I had also built a growing network of Indian expats in Berlin. This network became invaluable, not just in helping us settle in but also in creating a sense of belonging that is sometimes difficult to find as an immigrant.

If you're considering moving to Germany or any other European country of similar ilk, know that the initial phase can be challenging. There will be moments of doubt and hurdles to overcome. But with perseverance and a willingness to adapt, the experience can become incredibly rewarding, just as it did for us.

9

Continental Shift: A New World in Berlin

Sathya: *So how was the first year in Germany?*

Nambirajan: *Definitely it was as exhausting as climbing a mountain.*

Sathya: *But after a trek, there comes a feeling of fulfilling it. That is how I see it. How do you see it?*

Nambirajan: Yes, we crossed the tough first year. Now what's our long term plan?

Sathya: Long term plan is to stay and grow in Germany

Nambirajan: That is to get PR (Permanent Residency) and maybe citizenship in Germany?

Sathya: Or until Ranjana goes to her college for her undergraduate degree?

Nambirajan: Whichever is longer

Sathya: Also it's not just about just staying for a longer duration but to thrive and grow as a family during those years

Nambirajan: Agreed. The journey of a thousand miles begins with a single step

Sathya - Growing in Germany:

After about a year in Berlin, we began to embrace the German way of life. Sundays, known as *Ruhetag* (quiet day), when shops are closed, stopped being an inconvenience. Instead, we appreciated the opportunity to rest and spend time with family. The sustainable living culture of Germans—garbage segregation, recycling, and do-it-yourself household chores—became second nature to us. We stopped relying on delivery apps and started walking to buy groceries from nearby stores like Aldi, Rewe, and Lidl. After extensively using Olas and Uber cabs in India, we started using Berlin's exceptional public transport system, which costs only 49 euros a month for unlimited rides across buses, trains, and even ferries.

In Germany, there's no concept of hiring maids or servants; everyone does their own chores, from carpentry to household repairs. This meant we both had to figure out how to manage housework. Cleaning the house, cooking, washing clothes, and drying them were all split between the two of us. We also learned about many other nuances of German culture that might not be immediately evident to a tourist. For example, Germans have a deep respect for nature, evident in their *Schrebergärten* (small garden plots) where they grow fruits and vegetables. These plots are government-subsidized, encouraging green living. We even visited a few near our home and dreamt of having one such small garden home to use during the summer months. Slowly but surely, we were getting enrolled in Germany's way of living.

From a mother's perspective, Germany's Kita and school systems impressed me. Ranjana attended two different Kitas, where children learn through play. These institutions focus on developing motor skills through activities involving sand, water, and games. The concept of Kindergarten even originated in Germany. I never had to worry about cooking elaborate meals while juggling work, as the Kitas provided nutritious hot meals, breakfast, and snacks. Once, when I went to pick up Ranjana, the staff asked for my passport to verify my identity—such was their commitment to safety.

As Ranjana transitioned to school, the infrastructure and support systems amazed me. Public schools in Germany offer world-class facilities for free, and the daycare services ensure working parents can pick up their children after work. Schools teach respect for nature through visits to *Gartenarbeit Schule* (gardening school), preparing children to understand ecosystems and care for the environment. I even had ideas of creating similar gardening schools for children in India so they could connect to nature and learn preservation skills.

Another fantastic aspect of schools here is how they teach kids to be organized and independent from a young age—whether it's managing their files, traveling long distances by train, or learning to make their own meals. Their education system equips children with essential life skills. Some schools even have kitchens as laboratories.

There was a deep desire within me to work in Europe with distributed teams and diverse people, as I felt it would enhance my experience as a scrum master. I admire the professionalism in German work culture. Employees are treated with immense respect, and there are clear boundaries in the workplace. Every task involves thoughtful consideration rather than hasty decisions. At the same time, there's a perfect balance between work and life. It is safer for women to work, grow their families, and thrive here. With 28–30 vacation days a year and managers encouraging time off, I finally had time for myself and my family. I hadn't worked more than eight hours a day in the past two years, and the higher salary in Germany compared to India was just a bonus. I enjoy my job in Germany, and sometimes I travel to other cities for meetings. I'm fortunate to take my family along. My husband takes care of Ranjana while working from the hotel, and this helps me focus at my work. I believe this is the bare minimum every woman should expect—to grow in her career without missing out on her children. Germany understands families and the support systems they need better than many other countries.

We even used our free time to grow our YouTube channel, now called *Culture Konnect*. This creative project has strengthened my relationship with Nambi, turning everyday experiences into meaningful content and helping immigrants learn more about life in Germany.

In addition to our channel, we began traveling more thoughtfully, exploring history-rich places like Krakow in Poland and Marseilles in France. We became fans of free walking tours, a fantastic way to learn about the cities we visit. Our daughter, the youngest participant, has become a little traveler herself (Though she might now prefer playing in a *spielplatz* than going to a boring museum).

Berlin will always hold a special place in my heart for one significant reason: I found my Bharatanatyam guru here. Learning South Indian classical dance from a German teacher, Shebana Devi Akka, has been a dream come true. After seeing her performance as 'Devi' in Berlin in 2021, I joined her class, Natya Berlin, the following year. It's been a year since I became her student. Every Saturday, I attend her class, which has become a form of meditation for me. This dance form transcends logic and connects me to something greater. She is a selfless guru who always says, "Wake your body with your mind" to motivate me and shake off my laziness. Dance has helped me work on myself better. It helps me find inner balance and cope with my emotions. I believe art itself is a therapy. It helps combat stress that builds up in our body and improves our posture. Above all, it brings discipline to everyday life. Though I travel three hours to and from my class on Saturdays, it feels like an inward travel. My guru has studied under great teachers like the Dhananjayans in Chennai. I am blessed to have her as a guru, an ambassador for Bharatanatyam in Berlin.

With my Bharatanatyam guru - Shebana Devi akka

Beyond dance, we also started an initiative called *Let's Serve* with friends back home. Together, we sponsor the education of a child whose schooling was interrupted by COVID-19. It's a small contribution from our *Let's Serve* group, but I believe in the power of communities. These experiences have deepened my sense of responsibility and gratitude, reminding me of the importance of giving back.

Despite the hardships, the journey has been transformative. My struggles in the early days—growing up with an alcoholic father and leaving Madurai—have shaped who I am today. Now, through setbacks and challenges, we've found our way to work in Germany, a privilege I am deeply aware of. While working and raising my family here, I want to continue growing *Let's Serve*. If we can change the life of one child through our initiative, it will all be worth it. This is the fulfillment I've been seeking, the journey of a lifetime. As the saying goes, 'Whoever saves one life saves the world entire.'

Nambirajan - Working and Growing in Germany

Working in Germany has its own set of pros and cons. Having spent about a decade working in India, I've noticed significant differences between working there and in Germany. One of the most striking differences is the well-known 'work-life balance'. Back in India, I was accustomed to receiving work-related calls sometimes as late as 8 pm. Even during the festive season of Diwali, I was on a call late into the night. It seemed that the higher your salary, the more work hours they expected you to complete—a typical attitude that didn't have much emphasis on the effectiveness of work. In contrast, working in Germany has been a revelation. Over the past few years of work here, I've never received a work call after 5 pm. The automotive industry in Germany, where I'm employed, is particularly known for its steady pace of work.

Another notable difference is the level of pressure from top leadership. In one Indian startup I worked for, the CEO had a say in every minute detail of the product. In another firm, the Product Managers imposed tight timelines on the entire team which in turn would lead to the team scrambling to complete it, only for them to come and say that the whole project is scrapped. Such intense pressure is rare here. My interactions with the CEO are limited to town hall meetings, and while Product Managers do face business pressures, they don't heavily impact my work. The feedback also seems to be straight to the point of a typical, no-nonsense, no small talk approach that a typical German communication has.

There's also a distinct sense of integrity in the German workplace. Everything else being equal, German office environments seem to provide a space where integrity can thrive. In India, it often felt more about sincerity. Sometimes when I visit the Berlin office of my company, I see an elderly gentleman, working with a monk-like focus. Although I haven't spoken to him or even know his name, he embodies the German ethos of dedicated work and integrity that feels unique.

Lastly, the role of workers' unions and IG Metall stands out. In India, software workers generally lack unions that advocate for their rights. In Germany, however, IG Metall and the works council actively protect workers' rights and benefits. For instance, when Carieth (my current company) faced employee backlash over a planned reduction of 2,000 jobs last year, IG Metall and the works council quickly mobilized to inform employees of their rights and criticize the manner in which the news was handled. This active support contrasts sharply with the often impersonal way top executives in other countries might view their employees as mere 'resources' to be discarded if necessary. And thanks to IG Metall and workers council, many workers who might have otherwise been laid off, continue to work amidst the gloomy economic scenario in Germany.

Currently, as of November 2024, the economy is struggling to grow and layoffs are prevalent across Germany. FolksHagen recently said it intends to close a factory in Wolfsburg, leading to potential job losses. At my workplace, we're undergoing an 'efficiency program' that offers a voluntary exit bonus. From what I hear, many from the finance and HR teams have already opted for this exit, and there are talks of more departments being affected. Across many industries there are many layoffs as companies tighten their budget and find ways to cut costs and grow their profits. This dip in the German economy is partly attributed to the war between Ukraine and Russia that has been going on for more than 1000 days now. The war constrained the nation's energy dependence on Russia which was supplying enormous fuel that powered many of the industries in Germany. Even they provided for the heating gas that kept homes warm during the harsh winter season. This along with the rising inflation after Covid-19 has brought the German economy to a slow crawl - it has grown at a minuscule 0.08% in the last few quarters.

As I write this, there is also a political chaos that's growing. SPD (Social Democratic Party) and CDU (Christian Democratic Union) are two of the prominent parties in Germany and recently Olaf Scholz, the chancellor of Germany from the SPD party fired the Finance minister of Germany with whose party SPD had formed an alliance to form the government. Now that the government has lost its majority, there will be early elections in 2025. With the electoral win of Trump, and with many nations going a bit rightward, the next election might be won by CDU with significant wins for AFD (Alles fur Deutschland, a far-right wing party in Germany). And if this happens, the immigration level in Germany might be brought down - a move that has already been implemented in Canada by the Trudeau government.

Reflecting on the past few years, it's clear there have been two distinct economic phases in Germany from my point of view. From February 2022 to early 2023, the environment was vibrant, with thriving startups, active hiring, and less concern over budget control. From 2023 onwards, however, financial constraints have intensified, startups struggle for funding, and layoffs have become more common. For people who are planning to move to Germany for work, circa 2022 provided one of the best times with the hypothetical 'window for immigration' wide open with many companies hiring tech talent with the vibrant economy. And now in 2024, and probably 2025 - the downturn might have impacted immigration as well. And of course this doesn't mean people are coming to Germany with Chancenkarte (the new version of Job Seeker Visa) and then finding work here. It just means that the number of people finding a relevant opportunity to work and grow in Germany might have reduced.

Amid this uncertainty, during the last few months, I created a new version of Culture Konnect called **Career Konnect**. What started as a Whatsapp group for sharing referrals and discussing work trends, slowly continued to grow. We also had a meetup in Berlin at the Spiced Academy office where we had some talks from people who are working as data analysts and data scientists in Berlin. Career Konnect has emerged as a valuable space for people to seek referrals, expand their professional networks, and engage in career growth discussions. Our WhatsApp group of over 1000 members is a testament to the active and supportive conversations that keep the community vibrant. I am planning to take a few more initiatives to grow the community and to create opportunities for the people to grow and thrive in Germany.

On a personal note, I'm currently at a crossroad. Carieth is refocusing exclusively on automotive software, meaning that teams working on related software, like dealer related software and mobile applications, are being transferred to different teams within FolksHagen. Initially we had the opportunity to move to the KDX team, which is part of the FolksHagen conglomerate. But this transition fell through, with FolksHagen management preferring not to add new workers to its already straining economic resources. This created a new chaotic situation for us - which soon got resolved. Now my team has an opportunity to move to DTone (Another company in the FolksHagen universe. Some say there are about 1000 companies in the FolksHagen Universe). With design projects in Carieth reducing and the team shrinking slowly, I am now considering the move to DTone. This reminds me of the Robert Frost poem which I read during my childhood:

'Two roads diverged in a yellow wood,
And sorry I could not travel both

And be one traveler, long I stood
And looked down one as far as I could
To where it bent in the undergrowth.'

This transition situation feels eerily familiar though. Last year, I was deliberating over a move from Texad to Carieth, facing delays and uncertainties. Now, it's about transitioning to DTone and navigating similar uncertainties. There are a few differences though. While moving from Texad to Carieth, the entire team of 80+ people mostly opted in to move to Carieth, since it was clearly a better choice. With the move to DTone though, some people might opt to stay back in Carieth and the choice now is a bit more personal rather than at the company level. The road not taken is here to prompt a choice, and it's one I'll need to make. Whether this decision will be remembered with hope or regret in the future remains uncertain. Or rather I would have to make a choice and make it right - a more declarative and causing approach.

Traveling in Europe:

If you ask people like us who migrated from India to Europe why we moved, one of the common responses would be a variation of 'to explore Europe' or 'to experience a different culture.' Many of us share a passion for travel and discovering new places. The reasons may vary—whether to understand a location, experience a new way of life, or simply create some cool Instagram reels—but Europe, with its 27 countries and a plethora of uniquely different countries and cultures, is a traveler's dream. With historical landmarks, natural scenic spots, and cultural hubs, it's an adventure waiting to happen with every trip. Provided you have the right visa (Schengen), almost all of these countries are within reach.

Over the last few years of living in Europe, we've traveled to various places, mostly within Germany. Some of these trips have been full of joy, adding excitement and vibrancy to our lives, while others have helped us understand the origins of the word 'travails' —which, according to Google, means to 'engage in painful and laborious effort.' Whether enjoyable or difficult, here are some highlights from our travels.

From our different travel trips. Clockwise from the top - At Salzburg, Lavender garden in Aix en Provence, with Phyrge the mascot of Paris Olympics in Marseille and in a huge church carved inside a salt mine - The Wieliczka Salt Mine, Krakow, Austria

Marseille, France Trip: My love affair with the Olympics began in 1996. The Atlanta Olympics opening ceremony was the first one I watched live on TV, and at the very impressionable age of 10, I was mesmerized by the performances, the athletes' march, and the grandeur of the event. It was magical. I believe that was when the seed of wanting to witness the Olympics in person was planted.

Fast forward 28 years to January 2024, when my family and I were living in Berlin, and the Paris Olympics was set to happen in July. I missed out on the first batch of tickets but managed to secure tickets in February for two events: a football match in Marseille and a skateboarding/ breakdancing event at La Concorde in Paris. In hindsight, I regret not getting tickets for the beach volleyball event at the Eiffel Tower venue, which turned out to be one of the most iconic sites of the Paris Olympics.

However, my mistakes didn't end with the ticket bookings. I mistakenly booked my flight to Marseille for April 22 instead of July 22, which I only realized around July 19. I had booked the correct flights for my wife and child but not for myself. This error came about because I was trying to save on extra baggage fees. Trying to save 40 Euros only to lose 400 Euros. Definitely a smart move. After a frantic search for new flights, I ended up booking a two-leg journey with Lufthansa: Berlin to Düsseldorf, then Düsseldorf to Marseille. Thankfully, after a series of hurdles, we all boarded the same Ryanair flight and arrived in Marseille on July 22. Thinking of 'travails' of travel, this trip was one such even before it began.

In Marseille, we enjoyed a city walk before heading to our Airbnb, which turned out to be a pleasant stay. We also visited the nearby island Îles du Frioul and saw lavender fields in Aix-en-Provence. I watched the USA vs. France football match at the Marseille stadium, and afterward, we headed to Paris for more events. We also squeezed in a quick visit to the Nice beachfront, which turned out to be underwhelming since we spent less than two hours there.

On July 26, 2024, we found ourselves in Paris for the Olympic opening ceremony, where, in a break from tradition, the athletes marched along the Seine River instead of in a stadium. Although we didn't have tickets to the ceremony, we watched it from our Airbnb near Montlhéry, Paris. It rained that evening, and the ceremony unfolded across various iconic venues in Paris. We enjoyed it from the comfort of our Airbnb, with commentary from our French hosts. I was especially captivated by the horse that carried the Olympic torch along the Seine and the lighting of the final torch in a hot air balloon.

The next few days were spent exploring the famous sights of Paris, including the Eiffel Tower and the Palace of Versailles. We also attended a 3x3 basketball event at La Concorde after waiting in a long queue due to some organizational mishaps. After a few more days, we flew back to Berlin, bringing our Olympic adventure to an end. In retrospect, the hype surrounding watching the Olympics in person may be overrated. Perhaps it's best enjoyed on TV, like I did when I was 10.

Krakow, Poland trip: Travel has its own joys too, and that was certainly the case with our trip to Krakow in May 2024. Everything went smoothly: the flights were on time, the Airbnb was great, and the city was a delight to explore. The highlight was visiting the salt mines in Wieliczka, where we saw an entire church carved out of salt. Our tour guide shared fascinating stories about the mine's history, and we learned that the mine no longer produces salt. The revenue from salt production (2 million Euros) is dwarfed by the 200 million Euros it generates from tourism.

I also visited Auschwitz, the infamous concentration camp where thousands of Jews were subjected to horrific suffering and death in the hands of the Nazis. A few weeks earlier, I had watched 'The Zone of Interest', a moving portrayal about a Nazi family that lives right beside the Auschwitz camp and goes about their daily life even when monstrous evil goes on right beside. After having watched 'Schindler's List' and having read 'Maus' I was aware of some of the atrocities that happened during the Holocaust. Visiting Auschwitz made the atrocities all the more real. To go into the chambers where Jews were forced inside a chamber and a poisonous chemical called Zyklon was dropped from the top was a harrowing experience. Auschwitz is just one of many concentration camps that dot mainland Europe; Sachsenhausen, located near Berlin, is another one I hope to visit.

We also visited the Schindler's Factory Museum in Krakow, which is mostly dedicated to Poland's history but also tells the story of Oskar Schindler, a Nazi who saved hundreds of Jews by employing them in his factory. If you're unfamiliar with this part of German history, I highly recommend watching 'Schindler's List', an excellent film I first saw during my college days.

Salzburg and Hallstatt, Austria: Some trips are a mix of joy and disappointment. Our visit to Salzburg was wonderful—its small-town charm, nestled along a river, was captivating. We enjoyed a city walk where we learned about its rich history. However, Hallstatt, though picturesque, felt over hyped and overrun with Instagram tourists.

Prague and Barcelona: In addition to family trips, I've also traveled for work. I visited Prague for my company's year-end offsite and managed to explore the Dancing House and the Elevator of Death. I've been to Barcelona three times—first during a semester exchange, then for a company visit, and most recently for a workshop with SEAT Code. During these trips, I enjoyed local delicacies like *patatas bravas* and *paella*, and I visited iconic sites like the Sagrada Família, Camp Nou, and Parc Güell. The organic shapes and mosaics of Gaudi's architecture are a thing of beauty in Barcelona.

Our travels in Germany continue to this day. We are now planning for a visit to Weimar, the home of the Bauhaus design movement, which in turn inspired the teaching methodology of NID where I studied. Next we might visit Switzerland in 2025, ten years after my semester exchange years in Zurich. It would be great to visit those same places and to show them to my family. Also this might be the time to visit Interlaken which I missed during my semester exchange time. Great travel beckons and I hope to meet some of you in the journey ahead.

Adios Amigos.

10

Finding Home - Reflections on our journey

Sathya and Nambirajan: In the previous chapters, we provided our distinct opinions in separate sections. In this final chapter, we bring it all together as a common voice. There will be no separate sections from each of us. It's combined together into one.

Home is not just the brick and concrete building that houses people. At one level, it is also the place where you experience belonging. Home also has meaning beyond the usual brick and mortar building it usually refers to. This book, for example, has become a home for our story—a metaphysical home to our memories that helps connect with people like you, dear reader.

> *'Home is not where you are born. Home is where all your attempts to escape cease.'*

We recently came across these lines and we both started talking about it. Most of the time, 'Home' is not just the place where we were born or the place you grow up. 'Home' is the place, in our view, which we discover on our journey where you have a sense of belonging. We both were born in different cities in Southern India, moved for a brief stint to Northern India, and continued our work in Bengaluru before moving to Berlin. We have our home here in Germany now in a place that is way different from the many homes in India, and still we feel at home. Millions of immigrants before us and after us who move from one place to another continually adapt to their new environments and make their homes. Home in that way is more of a subtler mind-based psychological concept than a physical construct with brick and mortar or a geographical location with a latitude and longitude.

Delving a little deeper into the subtler aspects of home, it is also connected to our identities. And in that case as well, our identities have been amorphous. The particular identity of 'Tamils/Dravidian' began to diminish once we expanded our horizons and moved to North India to work there. And as 'software professionals' we became part of a bigger cosmopolitan culture in Bengaluru. And later on when we moved to Berlin, at the international level, our identities went beyond the usually defined 'Tamil speaking/software professional/Indian origin' labels. And despite all of this, we stay connected to our roots and continue our journeys.

Language is another identity which provides us 'Home'. Though we have moved to Berlin, we continue to watch Tamil movies and read about what is happening in Tamil Nadu. While we continue to learn German, our appreciation of Tamil culture continues. And at the same time, sometimes you can feel as a disconnected person in the place where you speak your mother tongue and feel at home in the place where the language is alien to you. That is the beauty of the world. We remember when we were stuck in a flood and went to a shelter without lights and even water for a night, a village akka who was sleeping next to us gave her only dry towel and lungi for Nambi to make us comfortable that night. I felt at home even in the darkness with her compassion. We still believe in this beautiful world and the beautiful fellow person who makes you feel at home. And in its countless forms—its love, compassion, and the warmth it offers—it is these that truly make a house a home.

> *'If you've lived your whole life in one country, you may never truly understand it.'*

Travel is another way to go beyond your own limitations of identities and to experience something new and different about ourselves and the world. When we travel, especially during those travels which are 'travails', we get to shed some of our identities and adopt new ones, for our own wellness and growth. Every time we travel, we make a conscious choice to shatter some parts of our rigidly defined identities and to say and experience that 'I'm still part of a bigger place'. While traveling for our work, conferences, and even for vacation, there is a learning curve with every place which has shaped us. In fact, travel makes a person more vulnerable to understanding the pain which the next-door friend goes through. We are all connected in a way, and travel helps you realize that the problems we encounter in our life journeys have a commonality.

Travel also helps us to consider the experiences of people whom we have never met as our own. When you realize some of the pain that your Bengali friend is going through and empathize with it, you gain access to understand similar human experiences when another friend is from Ukraine or Lebanon.

During crucial times like this with two wars ravaging our planet, 'Home' is also a political concept. The impact of these wars on people and their homes is well documented. During such wars, thousands of people move away from their country with the hope of creating a peaceful home in another country. People migrate away from their homes to give the best education and safety for their kids. People create new homes in new countries with the hope of getting back their peaceful sleep and to set up their families on a path of recovery and regeneration.

We're aware of how fortunate we are to have two homes, each offering something unique. The home we were born in, and the one we've come to call home after moving. Madurai, Tirunelveli, Bangalore, and India have all shaped us in ways we'll never forget, but Berlin is where we've finally found a place to rest. For now, Berlin is home. But who knows? Maybe that will change as we continue to explore.

We want to end this memoir with a Tamil saying that's often quoted: 'Yaadhum Oorae Yaavarum Kaelir' – 'Every place is my home, and everyone is my kin.'

It's a reminder that with love and compassion, we can make a place feel like home. The home we're looking for isn't out there, it's within us. When we find that peace within, we truly feel at home. And that's what we hope you find too.

Appendix 01

Hope you liked reading our book and if you would like to connect with us online, here are some links. Please scan them with your phone to access them

To watch our youtube channel Culture Konnect videos

To join Career Konnect Whatsapp channel – updates about jobs and career in Germany

Appendix 02

Here's a list of 10 'Dos and Donts' for people interested in moving to Germany, covering key things to do/ mistakes to avoid. Some of these mistakes we have made too, some are made by our friends and acquaintances and what we learnt online. We share them so you can learn from them.

1. Don't Fall for Rental Scams

Avoid paying deposits or signing contracts without visiting the apartment and verifying the landlord's identity. Cross-check details and be wary of deals that seem too good to be true. I knew people who sent 3000+ Euros to shady listings online and then struggled to retrieve the money.

2. Don't Overlook Local Rules

Familiarize yourself with recycling, noise restrictions (Ruhezeiten), and other German regulations. There are also regulations for the amount of gold you can bring to Germany. Please check in the customs (Zoll) official portal for updated rules. Violating them can lead to fines or conflicts with neighbors. Again here we know of people who had to pay hefty fines because they carried gold beyond limit while flying from India and didn't declare.

3. Don't Assume English Will Suffice Everywhere

While many Germans speak English, learning basic German phrases is crucial for daily interactions, especially with authorities and in rural areas. Incase if you have a child who goes to public school, knowing *ein bisschen Deutsch* (a little German) can be useful in helping them with their homework, attending school meetings and so on. Also if you plan to stay in Germany for long term, studying German helps in integrating better.

4. Don't Forget to Open a Local Bank Account

By local bank account, I mean a bank account with IBAN number that starts with 'DE'. Though neo-banks like Revolut might provide a quick access to new bank accounts they have LT IBAN number and aren't ideal for long term use. German banking is necessary for paying rent, bills, and receiving salaries. Some landlords may only accept SEPA bank transfers.

5. Don't Ignore Tax Responsibilities

Register for a Tax Identification Number (Steuer-ID) and understand local tax obligations, especially if you're employed or freelancing. Radio tax is a small contribution that you need to make every month. Do take some time to understand it and get this tax payment right.

6. Don't Underestimate paperwork

German bureaucracy can be slow and demanding. Prepare all necessary documents in advance, and keep both physical and digital copies. I made the mistake of not keeping my salary slips and the small green paper which accompanies a blue card - don't make that mistake. Germans love paperwork and if you become good at it, that will make your life easier in Germany.

7. Don't Forget Cultural Differences

Germans value punctuality, planning, and directness. Respect these cultural norms to integrate better and avoid misunderstandings.

8. Don't Miss Out on Public Transportation Cards

Avoid buying single tickets repeatedly. Get a monthly or annual public transport pass (e.g., BVG in Berlin) for significant savings and convenience. And incase if you get a fine, pay it early.

9. Do consider sustainable living

Berlin has a store called Humana which specialises in selling second-hand clothes. Germans are also big into sorting waste and disposing home waste properly. Learn about these to get better at them.

10. Do plan ahead for Sundays and Public Holidays:

Most stores are closed on Sundays and public holidays. Stock up on essentials beforehand to avoid inconvenience. Germans plan for holidays even a year in advance whereas desis do it typically just a month in advance. Planning in advance can help keep your travel costs lesser and smoother.

And incase if you come to Germany, send us a 'hi'.

www.ingramcontent.com/pod-product-compliance
Lightning Source LLC
LaVergne TN
LVHW091313150826
845673LV00006B/1636